News Journalism and Twitter

This book provides a critical account of the impact of Twitter on journalism, exploring how the news media has adapted to and normalised the use of the platform in the industry.

Offering a comprehensive understanding of Twitter uses for journalistic purposes, this book explores the platform's use as a 'global village', as an ambient news environment, and as a global marketplace. Drawing on two empirical case studies (United Kingdom and Greece), Dagoula examines academic conceptualisations of Twitter, journalists' self-perceptions, and uses of the platform by a variety of media outlets and journalists. Adopting an evolutionary approach known as punctuated equilibrium, which consists of three stages of disruption, adaption, and normalisation, the author reveals the costs and benefits of Twitter's impact on both the institutional values and practices of news journalism today.

News Journalism and Twitter is an invaluable resource for researchers and students of digital journalism and media studies.

Chrysi Dagoula is an Assistant Professor at the Centre for Media and Journalism Studies, University of Groningen, Netherlands.

Disruptions: Studies in Digital Journalism
Series editor: Bob Franklin

Disruptions refers to the radical changes provoked by the affordances of digital technologies that occur at a pace and on a scale that disrupts settled understandings and traditional ways of creating value, interacting and communicating both socially and professionally. The consequences for digital journalism involve far-reaching changes to business models, professional practices, roles, ethics, products and even challenges to the accepted definitions and understandings of journalism. For Digital Journalism Studies, the field of academic inquiry which explores and examines digital journalism, disruption results in paradigmatic and tectonic shifts in scholarly concerns. It prompts reconsideration of research methods, theoretical analyses and responses (oppositional and consensual) to such changes, which have been described as being akin to 'a moment of mind-blowing uncertainty'.

Routledge's book series, *Disruptions: Studies in Digital Journalism*, seeks to capture, examine and analyse these moments of exciting and explosive professional and scholarly innovation which characterize developments in the day-to-day practice of journalism in an age of digital media, and which are articulated in the newly emerging academic discipline of Digital Journalism Studies.

News Journalism and Twitter
Disruption, Adaption and Normalisation
Chrysi Dagoula

Digital Journalism and the Facilitation of Hate
Gregory P. Perreault

For more information about this series, please visit: www.routledge.com/Disruptions/book-series/DISRUPTDIGJOUR

News Journalism and Twitter
Disruption, Adaption and Normalisation

Chrysi Dagoula

LONDON AND NEW YORK

First published 2023
by Routledge
4 Park Square, Milton Park, Abingdon, Oxon OX14 4RN

and by Routledge
605 Third Avenue, New York, NY 10158

Routledge is an imprint of the Taylor & Francis Group, an informa business

© 2023 Chrysi Dagoula

The right of Chrysi Dagoula to be identified as author of this work has been asserted in accordance with sections 77 and 78 of the Copyright, Designs and Patents Act 1988.

All rights reserved. No part of this book may be reprinted or reproduced or utilised in any form or by any electronic, mechanical, or other means, now known or hereafter invented, including photocopying and recording, or in any information storage or retrieval system, without permission in writing from the publishers.

Trademark notice: Product or corporate names may be trademarks or registered trademarks, and are used only for identification and explanation without intent to infringe.

British Library Cataloguing-in-Publication Data
A catalogue record for this book is available from the British Library

ISBN: 9781032139760 (hbk)
ISBN: 9781032139807 (pbk)
ISBN: 9781003231776 (ebk)

DOI: 10.4324/9781003231776

Typeset in Times New Roman
by codeMantra

To my family.
For their unconditional love and support.

Contents

List of figures ix
List of tables xi
Acknowledgements xiii

Introduction 1

1 **The two dominant views of Twitter and news journalism** 7
 1.1 Twitter as enabling and benefiting news journalism 7
 1.2 Twitter as distorting news journalism 17

2 **Punctuated equilibrium: disruption, adaption and normalisation** 29
 2.1 The institution of news journalism and punctuated equilibrium 29
 2.2 Disruption as a commonplace event 39

3 **What news journalists say about their uses of Twitter** 52
 3.1 Qualitative approach: research interviews 52
 3.2 Questionnaire themes concerning the evolutionary impact of Twitter on news journalism 53
 3.3 Journalists' evaluation of Twitter's costs and benefits to news journalism 67

4 **From disruption to normalisation: journalists' accounts on Twitter (2009–2021)** 75
 4.1 An account of the participants 76
 4.2 The participants' first Tweets: 2009–2011 76

4.3 The 'presentation of self': how the participants chose to display their biographical information 80
4.4 Account core features: account activity, use of hashtags and mentions and formatting tweets and textual choices 86

5 **An evaluation of the direct and indirect costs and benefits of Twitter to news journalism** 105

References 111
Index 121

Figures

2.1	Main thesis	33
2.2	Disruption, adaption, normalisation: example 1	34
2.3	Disruption, adaption, normalisation: example 2	36
4.1	Journalists' popularity versus journalists' activity on Twitter	88
4.2	Journalists' activity on Twitter (2009–2021)	89
4.3	Journalists' use of hashtags compared to total number of tweets (2009–2021)	92
4.4	Journalists' use of hashtags (2009–2021)	93
4.5	Journalists' use of mentions compared to total amount of tweets (2009–2021)	96
4.6	Journalists' use of mentions (2009–2021)	96

Tables

2.1	Categorisation of journalists based on their uses and perceptions of Twitter (from the most resistant to less).	44
3.1	List of journalists interviewed	52
4.1	Participants' work profile, gender and followers	77
4.2	Explicit awkwardness in first Tweets	79
4.3	Journalists' self-presentation on Twitter	82
4.4	Account core features	87

Acknowledgements

I am grateful to Professor Bob Franklin, editor of the series *Disruptions: Studies in Digital Journalism*, for his encouragement, guidance and support while developing this book. I also owe a debt of gratitude to all participating journalists for their time and for sharing their thoughts, insights and experiences with me. I would also like to extend my warmest thanks to my colleagues at the Centre for Media and Journalism Studies, University of Groningen. Last, but not least, I cannot thank my family and friends enough for accompanying me on this journey, and for always being there for me. I consider myself incredibly lucky to have you by my side.

Introduction

Twitter was officially launched in July 2006.[1] It gained substantial popularity in March 2007, when it debuted its full version at 'South by Southwest' (SXSW) – a popular music festival and conference, populated by technology connoisseurs. The increase in activity during the conference (from 20.000 to 60.000 messages per day)[2] translated to venture capital that led to its establishment as a corporate company. Twitter's popularity soon surpassed that of Jaiku, one of the first microblogging platforms (Ebner & Schiefner, 2008), and it quickly became the 'undisputed leader' among those platforms (Mayfield, 2008, p. 6). From February to April 2008, U.S. traffic to the site nearly doubled to approximately 1.2 million people per month (Honeycutt & Herring, 2009). By mid-2007, international media outlets such as the BBC and the New York Times, and politicians like Barack Obama were using the platform (Burgess & Baym, 2020). By 2013, Twitter had more than 200 million active users who were collectively sending 400 million tweets every day (Standage, 2013). In addition, the platform was widely endorsed by news outlets. However, compared to platforms, such as Facebook, Twitter's numbers have remained relatively small.[3] As Burgess and Baym (2020, p. 10) note 'Twitter has retained a loyal core user base and has grown steadily, particularly internationally, but it has consistently lacked the stratospheric year-on-year user growth demanded by investors and shareholders'. Even so, from the beginning, Twitter presented itself as a distinct platform with its own social networking culture, that emphasised two things: 'a simple social technology' that allowed individuals to connect with friends, whilst becoming part of 'an informational public communication platform' (Burgess & Baym, 2020, p. 12). Burgess and Baym (2020) refer to this tension as enabling Twitter to produce its unique culture.

Twitter is characterised by two key features. Firstly, it is an open, user-centred, social networking space in which profiles can be public

DOI: 10.4324/9781003231776-1

2 *Introduction*

and unlocked, and accessible to anyone, registered or non-registered (Huberman et al., 2008). Secondly, it requires its users to express themselves laconically and develop short-hand expressions and discourse markers in their communicative exchanges (Bruns, 2018). Its first version, called Twttr, was based on mobile-phone text messaging and consisted of a website that displayed updates from users in one public timeline. This technical requirement set a limitation of 140 characters for users' tweets – a limitation that, along with the openness of the network, defined part of its culture. In 2017, the character count of a tweet was increased to 280. At first, this 'concision requirement' generated banal messages about users' everyday activities, though there were already signs of its potential as an 'early warning system'. An example of this was the reporting of an earthquake evidenced by Biz Stone's, one of Twitter's co-founders, first blog post about Twitter, where he refers to how an earthquake led to the 'twittering' of reports.[4] Gradually, Twitter appealed to newsrooms and journalists alike. The 'concision requirement' which allowed for snippets of information to be circulated in the platform contributed to this, but also to its successful employment during crises.[5] From this early usage until today, Twitter is being used as a 'global newsroom', the 'go-to site for journalists seeking to follow the flow of information' (Burgess & Baym, 2020, p. 10) and to such an extent that today one can hear talk of 'media Twitter' and its adoption by news media is prolific and universal. In short, Twitter has moved from banal chatter to carrying the news.

The argument and evidence that unravel here is concerned to understand the nature and extent of Twitter's influence on news journalism. Views on Twitter's impact on news journalism vary and range from arguments that emphasise: encouraging citizen participation and audience involvement (Artwick, 2013; Hermida, 2012; Murthy, 2013, 2018; Vis, 2013); improving the sourcing of news stories, information quality and news gathering (Barnard, 2016; Johnson et al., 2018; Gulyas, 2013, McGregor & Molyneux, 2020; Mourão, 2015); speeding up the news cycle and transforming the architecture of the news (from printing to sharing) (Broersma & Graham, 2016; Hedman, 2016; Hermida, 2016; Papacharissi, 2015; Revers, 2015); facilitating an ambient news environment (Hermida, 2010, 2013, 2014); to degrading information quality and facilitating extreme views dominated by misinformation and disinformation (Aral, 2020; Howard, 2020; Wardle & Derakhsan, 2017; Wardle, 2020); prompting trivia, engendering self-censorship (Dagoula, 2017), encouraging intra-elite debates and reinforcing so-called echo-chambers (Bail, 2021; Dagoula, 2019; Dubois & Blank, 2018; Maares et al., 2020); distorting the public sphere (Bouvier &

Rosenbaum, 2020; Fuchs, 2013; Theocharis et al., 2016); and facilitating the harassment and abuse of journalists (e.g., Toxic Twitter)[6] (Franklin & Canter, 2019; Lewis et al., 2020; Nelson, 2021; Standage, 2013). Chapter 1 opens the book by collating and reviewing these accounts in a systematic and theoretically coherent way under the rubric of two dominant views: first, Twitter as enabling and benefiting news journalism; second, Twitter as distorting news journalism.

These two views are sub-divided into further categories. The first view is divided into a perception of Twitter as an ambient news environment; as a 'global village'; and as benefiting news journalism. A second perception of the Twitter platform is divided into Twitter's effect on professional pressures; as underpinning information disorder and Twitter as ideally suited to mediate populism and the coarsening of political and civil discourse which devalues journalism. Chapter 2 suggests that answering the question about the real nature of Twitter's impact on news journalism requires a resort to evolutionary theory conceived in terms of a process of punctuated equilibrium. This approach derives from insights from evolutionary biology and social policy to provide the optimal way to understand Twitter[7] and its impact on the institution of news journalism.

It is well understood in sociology that institutions seek to institutionalise (socialise) their constituent organisations and correspondingly the members of those organisations, into a consistently held set of norms and mores that define how to undertake a role in that profession, or job. To claim that Twitter has brought major changes to the institution of news journalism, it is important to understand such changes as both institutional and behavioural. The significant question here is whether the norms and mores of the institution of news journalism have changed to such an extent that traditionally held professional norms have altered prompting a shift in the ways of going about being a news journalist and creating news journalism. In essence, has Twitter disrupted the institution of news journalism to produce new practices and forms of news journalism, and thereby altered the core of news journalism practice? These are empirical questions which were addressed in an analysis which involved a study of 49 journalists,[8] how they used Twitter and what they thought its impact was on news journalism.

Specifically, this research involved interviews with 22 journalists from Greece and the United Kingdom about their uses of Twitter during the period of 2017–2022 (Chapter 3) supported by longitudinal research which examined 27 journalists' Twitter accounts over an 11-year period, 2009–2021 (Chapter 4). Both chapters provide

4 *Introduction*

an empirical account of how these news journalists understand the impact of Twitter upon their practices, norms, mores and professional routines to establish an empirically rich account of how they actually use Twitter. These two chapters also provide an empirical account of 'punctuated equilibrium' through a qualitative study (research interviews) with news journalists that explores what they say about their use of Twitter, and an evolutionary account by analysing how journalists Twitter accounts have changed over the period of 2009–2021. Consequently, Chapter 3 examines journalists' views and personal accounts of their use of Twitter holistically and how their experiences accord with the process of disruption, adaption and normalisation. Whilst Chapter 4 consists of an analysis of journalists' accounts on Twitter (2009–2021) by following the three stages of punctuated equilibrium discussed in Chapter 2. In combination, the two chapters allow us to trace journalists' perceptions of Twitter in evolutionary terms as well as thematically, thereby providing an assessment of the net benefits and costs of Twitter to the institution and practices of news journalism.

This empirical requirement is necessary (Vollmer, 2013, p. 227) because 'exploring punctuated equilibrium begins with pieces of evidence of drastic change and then goes on to establish the particular processes and disruptions accounting for this drastic change'. Therefore, there is a need to establish processes accounting for the rapid transformations of empirical measures. Baumgartner and Jones (2009), who adapted the theory of punctuated equilibrium to social policy, underline empirical research (and preferably one that combines more than one approach) as means to understand the processes of disruption, adaption and normalisation through the lens of punctuated equilibrium. To this end, they particularly encourage 'longitudinal sectional comparisons of a single issue over time'. Therefore, this book takes this as its chosen methodological design to understand the processes of disruption, adaption and normalisation through the evolutionary lens of punctuated equilibrium.

Overall (both in theoretical and empirical terms), this book attempts to offer a comprehensive account of Twitter's impact on news journalism. My thesis throughout is that this impact occurs in the context of a constant state of punctuated equilibrium. In essence, what we have is an evolutionary pattern which when applied to news journalism reveals both the direct and indirect costs and benefits to the changing practices of news journalism, and which best explains the impact of Twitter on news journalism (Chapter 5). Consequently, change is here assessed in two ways: first, the costs and benefits of Twitter in relationship to the institution of news journalism and its institutional values and norms, and second, the costs and benefits of Twitter in relation to professional behavioural change in terms of how news journalism is practiced.

Throughout this book, Twitter is considered as part of a media ecosystem that allows 'for the emergence of new, more flexible means of providing news' (Picard, 2014, p. 277). In other words, it needs to be remembered that the arguments that follow do not assume that Twitter is the sole causal determinant of social or institutional change in news journalism, rather, Twitter, is part of a range of communicative options. Accordingly, whilst Twitter is the centre of attention for this book, I am not saying that Twitter is a singularly special force that accounts for the process of punctuate equilibrium as it played out through the impact of new communication technologies replacing old communication technologies and all that went with that. Rather, it needs to be remembered that Twitter is part of a broader platform ecosystem that is subject to evolutionary change. In that sense, Twitter is part of an array of advances in information and communication technology that has 'fundamentally transformed the structural conditions of communication' (Mounk, 2018, p. 139), the significance of which is widely studied. But we still need to state the obvious, though frequently neglected, view that in evolutionary terms the process of punctuated equilibrium brings with it an understanding of the range of interconnected benefits and costs that Twitter has brought to the standing and practice of news journalism.

Notes

1 An account of Twitter's biography includes a story about its beginning and its founders and it tends to be as confusing as any story of an I.T. company that encompasses experiments, creative outputs and of course, business models. Twitter started as 'a SMS of the Internet' or 'a short message service, a phone call, an e-mail and a blog: less cumbersome than keeping a blog, less exclusive than talking to one person on a phone, less formal than e-mail exchange and less elaborate than most SNSs' (van Dijck, 2012, p. 3); however, what is important here is (a) its scale and (b) its impact on news journalism.
2 Calore, M. (2007, 9 March). *Twitter is Ruling SXSW*. TheWired. https://www-wired-com.proxy-ub.rug.nl/2007/03/twitter-is-ruling-sxsw/
3 By the end of 2021 (fourth quarter of 2021), Facebook had 2.91 billion monthly active users, while its revenue reached more than 85 billion US dollars (*Statista*, 2021).
4 Stone, B. (2006, August 3). *Have Your Quake and Twitter It Too*. Twitter Blog https://blog.twitter.com/en_us/a/2006/have-your-quake-and-twitter-it-too
5 Even from its early years, Twitter contributed significantly to the reporting of crises or breaking news (Farhi 2009), such as the earthquake in China (2008), the fires in California (2008), the earthquake in New Zealand

6   *Introduction*

(2011). The phenomenon of using Twitter during these types of events is the main theme of several works. Amanda Lee Hughes and Leysia Palen (2009) referred to its dynamic during emergencies, Bibi Van der Zee (2009) discussed its potential to "triumph" as a medium during protests, Lev Grossman (2009) drawing on the Iranian Elections of 2009 underlines its substance in countries where censorship predominates. With reference to Twitter's early days, Mills et al. (2007) question whether the immediacy in responding from the first moment an event occurs is translated to information quality. In their study, they show that Twitter transcends mainstream journalism online during the first 24 hours, after which mainstream media have the leading role.

6 Amnesty International. (2018). https://www.amnesty.org/en/latest/research/2018/03/online-violence-against-women-chapter-1/
7 The process of punctuated equilibrium is derived from social policy (Baumgartner & Jones, 2009) which in turn is derived from evolutionary biology (Eldredge & Gould, 1972; Gould, 1982; Vollmer, 2013). See also: Givel (2010).
8 This study examines professional news journalism. Professionalism is a normative ideal and should be approached as 'a sociological category of analysis to study how journalism defines itself in society vis-à-vis other occupations, professions and areas of activity' (Waisbord, 2013, pp. 3–4). Therefore, in relation to news journalism, it is news organisations (both legacy and net-native) that comprise its institutional base, with journalists being a professional group that shares a common code of professional values. In other words, it is a professional group that regards itself as having institutional standing manifest in and through codes of behaviour, ethical standards, self-regulation, editorial codes, codes of conduct, professional bodies and associations and so on. The panoply and trappings of professional normative power serves to define how news journalism should be undertaken and accordingly the standards which should be upheld.

1 The two dominant views of Twitter and news journalism

Twitter is a communicative environment that enables a variety of communicative acts, ranging from the expression of the 'discursive self' (Dayter, 2016) to social and political discourse. Journalists' 'cultures of use' of Twitter shape the platform, and conversely, Twitter's multifunctionality and scale of use influence news journalism. To best understand Twitter's impact on changes affecting the institution of news journalism requires that we examine the two dominant views of Twitter as first enabling and benefiting news journalism, and second of Twitter as distorting and representing a cost to news journalism. The first view regards Twitter as a communicative space that provides an ambient news environment and constitutes a global village within which news journalism flourishes amidst diverse empowered audiences. The second view embraces three basic arguments: (a) Twitter causes irreconcilable professional pressures; (b) Twitter underpins information disorder; and (c) Twitter is ideally suited to mediate populism and the coarsening of political and civil discourse and devalues journalism.

1.1 Twitter as enabling and benefiting news journalism

1.1.1 Twitter as an ambient news environment

Discussions on Twitter's enabling impact on news journalism assume two forms: first that Twitter created an ambient news environment that somehow replaced traditionally structured news cycles, and second that Twitter took the form of a global village that in part facilitated the emergence of what Silverstone (2007) refers to as the rise of 'mediapolis', essentially a benign mediated ethical space of equal expression for the working out of our invariant civil concerns (Harrison, 2019a).

8 *The two dominant views of Twitter and news journalism*

In 2006, one of Twitter's developers, Biz Stone, set the tone about the use of Twitter as a warning or alert system. Following up this way of thinking about Twitter, Hermida (2010) suggested understanding Twitter as providing us with an ambient or peripheral awareness consisted of two elements: that Twitter alerts us to the fact that an event is happening, and that at the same time Twitter condenses a representation of that event. In this light, he further argues that Twitter is an awareness system that 'facilitates the immediate dissemination of digital fragments of news information from official and unofficial sources over a variety of systems and devices'. Drawing on studies in computer science, Hermida (2010, p. 298) regards new communication technologies such as Twitter as 'broad, asynchronous, lightweight, and always-on communication systems [which] are creating new kinds of interactions around the news and are enabling citizens to maintain a mental model of news and events around them'. For Hermida (2010, p. 298), the introduction of Twitter provided journalists 'with more complex ways of understanding and reporting on the subtleties of public communication', in direct contrast to traditional journalism that 'defines fact as information and quotes from official sources, which in turn has been identified as forming the vast majority of news and information content'.

This early analysis of Twitter's impact on news journalism highlights the ways that Twitter benefits news journalism, namely facilitates immediacy, enables the co-creation of news, and provides an arena that always contains news. The ambient news environment facilitated by Twitter consists both of messages read in the foreground and a slew of messages which are not read or engaged with, but which exist in the background. For news journalists and news audiences, this information dynamic of engagement and non-engagement endures constantly over time and helps to create what Hermida refers to as a mental portrait of news events (2010, p. 301). While this type of information dynamic can be challenging for users, because it requires that they need to constantly filter and check information, it can simultaneously provide an opportunity for journalists to 'help the public negotiate and regulate the flow of awareness information, providing tools that take account of this new mode for the circulation of news. Journalists would be seen as sense-makers, rather than just reporting the news' (Hermida, 2010, p. 304).

Understood in this way, Twitter is seen as an ambient news environment that influences news journalism's routines and practices when sourcing and disseminating the news. Since it not only facilitates the immediate dissemination and reception of short fragments of information from a variety of formal and informal sources, but it also 'creates social awareness streams that provide a constantly updated, live representation of the experiences, interests and opinions of users' (Papacharissi, 2014, p. 360), where the news is 'collaboratively constructed out of subjective experience, opinion, and emotion, all sustained by and sustaining ambient news environments' (Papacharissi, 2015, p. 34). Perhaps predictably, this view led to numerous discussions about the need to also understand whether this entailed a new form of journalism. For Hermida (2012, p. 311), this is 'ambient' journalism, which 'conceptualises journalism as a tele-mediated practice and experience driven by networked, always-on communication technologies and media systems of immediacy and instantaneity'. According to this view, journalism becomes 'fragmented, omnipresent, and ingrained in the everyday media experiences of users, with contributions from both professionals and non-professionals' (Hermida, 2012, p. 311). Twitter as an ambient news environment emphasises users' incidental and fragmented exposure to news.

Twitter users, and more specifically those who follow media and journalistic accounts, are constantly exposed to a diversity of news, consisting of either information or commentary. Because of this, it was suggested that this constant and incidental exposure affected users' perception and hence their understanding of the news and of news journalism. Bruns (2012, p. 3) discusses Twitter as undermining the masthead and as serving to atomise the news, while users move towards a 'news will find me' mentality, which subsequently increases the opportunity to receive news from a wider variety of news outlets. Johnson (2009) refers to a 'customised newspaper' reminiscent of Negroponte's 'Daily Me' (1995), where each user has the opportunity to receive an 'eclectic mix of news and information', but also to be constantly aware 'of what others in a user's network are reading and consider important' (Hermida, 2010, p. 303).

In sum, the benefits to news journalism were perceived to be that in and through news becoming a 'Twitter-centred ambient news environment', Twitter brought to the fore the possibilities for journalists to enhance awareness, to build a more intelligent public sphere with the capacity for what John Dewey referred to as social inquiry (in essence a problem-solving public) and to reference the views of a more diverse audience than previously – an audience that reflected their views and interests. All of which could take advantage of the instantaneous nature of Twitter and its inherently plural (and widespread) adoption.

10 *The two dominant views of Twitter and news journalism*

1.1.2 Twitter as a 'global village'

The second dominant view is that 'Twitter can be viewed as accelerating the reach of McLuhan's global village' (Murthy, 2013, p. 20). Murthy's reference to McLuhan highlights the view that the process of 'new electronic interdependence' 'recreates the world in the image of a global village' (1962, p. 31). A metaphor that emphasises the proximity and familiarity of a village with the mediated circumstances and conditions we currently live in and which due to the widespread adoption of media technologies has generated a highly interconnected world. The metaphor is certainly helpful as a generality which emphasises connectedness and public intimacy as well as the interconnection of the personal and the social. Here it is more useful when understood in terms of the way it conceptualises Twitter's impact on news journalism.

When applied to Twitter and news journalism, the metaphor fosters a series of promises. Firstly, it encompasses and tames globalisation as consisting of the 'far-flung' and disparate, by suggesting that Twitter is a global network that overcomes unfamiliarity, distance and otherness into a network which can be managed and which brings people together. Secondly, it highlights the aspect of connectedness by presenting Twitter as an open network that facilitates freedom (from state intervention) and personal networking. Thirdly, the metaphor underscores the primary role of increased understanding, commonality and sympathy for others in the village. In this, it emphasises idealised form of associative civil life.

Combined these promises point to different types or forms of 'journalistic sociality' (ways of being conceived of as being the modern equivalent of a local village reporter) within the platform. These three promises also emphasise enhanced audience interaction, participation and democratic control. The metaphor of 'village life' brings with it the requirements for the self-performance of public images and how to manage them when engaging with other villagers. For Murthy (2013, p. 21) though the real significance of the metaphor is the potential for far-flung individuals to be connected to an immersive global network and to have their voices amplified exponentially.

However, what some have thought missing from this conception of Twitter (as a form of global village) is alluded to in the adjacent metaphor of a 'global marketplace' (Shah, 2008). The metaphor of 'global marketplace' points to the benefits of Twitter to journalism by focusing on what we can summarily call commercial sustainability, and by placing the emphasis on commercial benefits to news organisations – both how they can stay in business and improve their business. The global marketplace is frequently claimed to have generated benefits that span a news organisation's ability to know its audience, refine and extend its services, introduce metrics and analytics into newsrooms and for journalists to develop niche information services. Incidentally, for some journalists, Twitter as a global market place also represents an opportunity for self-branding and promotion and (presumably) commercial enhancement. However, it remains the case that whatever the metaphor the emphasis is on global reach, public intimacy and improved journalism of the kind given by Twitter becoming an ambient news environment – one that envelops 'village life'.

1.1.3 Twitter as benefiting news journalism

By bringing together these two conceptualisations, Twitter as an ambient news environment and Twitter assuming the form of a global village, a list of five interconnected ways that Twitter benefits news journalism emerges.

1.1.3.1 The new audience

The first way concerns the shift from a broadcast audience to a networked audience (Marwick & boyd, 2010). Networked audience refers to an abstract group of new and diverse publics. These 'new' audience consist of real and potential viewers for digital content that are connected not only to the product or the user that produces that product, but also to each other in an active, communicative network, that relies on the presumption of personal authenticity and connection (Marwick & boyd, 2010, p. 129). Personal authenticity is established in the ways views are expressed, in the manners of expression, as well as in the language used. This audience exists within a larger social demographic and contains many different social relationships to be navigated (Marwick & boyd, 2010, pp. 129–130). The advantage this 'new' audience has over its antecedent broadcast audience is that it can communicate with the speaker directly.

The benefits to journalism of a 'new' audience, that is much more connected, is that it is considered to offer journalists and media organisations opportunities to expand their target groups by connecting with young and affluent audiences (Messner et al., 2011, p. 8). Broersma and Graham (2012, p. 404) describe 'a permanent exchange' that takes place between all parties on Twitter, as 'the interaction between journalists, sources and members of the public is triangulated' offering them the opportunity 'to step in and (re-)distribute, respond, and comment continuously'. These early studies reveal an enthusiasm for Twitter which was heralded a 'game changer' for newsrooms, with 'the power to connect reporters and sources, as well as readers, like never before' (Artwick, 2013, p. 212). These changes allowed journalism to be less of a product and more of a service that serves citizens by directly responding to their questions and concerns. This 'question and answer' approach suggests that journalism is shifting towards a form of public dialogue and discursive civility, less reliant on received top-down news or elite or official sources (Artwick, 2013, p. 212; Hermida, 2010, p. 298). Spatially conceived, Twitter is 'a hybrid space for the cultural production of journalism, with a broad range of actors involved in the filtering, framing and interpretation of news' (Hermida, 2016, p. 410) that, according to Barnidge et al. (2020, p. 407), has led to the reshaping of professional journalistic norms through the 'encouragement of higher levels of social interaction and reciprocal collaboration with audience members'. This 'enhanced interaction' with audiences led to Hermida's (2013; Hermida et al., 2011) conceptualisation of this 'new audience' and of Twitter's users as 'active recipients': essentially as audiences that are expected to act promptly when news is happening and to actively react when news is published – to act as observers and sources reacting to newsworthy events at the start of the journalistic process, and to then adopt an interpretive role as commentators who share and discuss the published material. It is also considerations and expectations of this kind that took place in scholarly debates and concerned blogs during the early 2000s. For instance, Singer's (2003) 'who is a journalist' and Gillmor's (2004, as cited in Jardin, 2004) 'we are all journalists now' capture an optimistic tendency that points to the 'dramatic blurring of boundaries' between journalists and 'those formerly known as media audiences' (Rosen, 2006; Shapiro, 2014, p. 556). In other words, connectivity became the central characteristic and primary feature for journalists and their audiences. It also became the legitimation, the raison d'être (and a business model) for social networking platforms like Twitter.

1.1.3.2 News gathering

The second positive effect that was argued for concerned the changes that occurred in journalists' news gathering practices. Bruno (2011, p. 8) compares the 'Twitter effect' to the 'CNN effect' noting that 'just as the "CNN effect" was crucial in centring media and political attention on a global crisis', the 'Twitter effect' makes similar promises by 'offering a more in-depth coverage of natural disasters

The two dominant views of Twitter and news journalism 13

and "forgotten" wars'. Twitter achieves this by providing 'visibility to threatened voices and political protests in less democratic countries' and by quickly spreading 'information regarding upcoming catastrophes and/or current health pandemics'. This reflects the opportunities for live coverage without having any reporters on the ground, as newsgathering can consist of the collection of user-generated content that is available in the platform. This benefit is seen as particularly important during breaking news events (Vis, 2013). Social media sourcing is regarded as allowing journalists to enrich their stories, to amplify their scope, and to retain or even enhance 'the degree of authenticity' as journalists can be close to where the story is happening (Gulyas, 2013, p. 271). To this end, social networks are considered as 'huge pools of "collective intelligence"' (Broersma & Graham, 2012, p. 404). Jarvis (2019) sees Twitter as helping journalists connect to people that would not potentially prioritise in their reporting. For instance, at the time of the pandemic, the platform was recognised for the way it allowed journalists to rapidly assess situations and to call attention to specific matters (Lieberman, 2021).

In this process of live and/or crisis coverage, users work on a story alongside journalists, but also independently by going through the process of 'gatewatching' as Bruns (2005) calls it, in which they 'identify and link to relevant material found elsewhere online, as well as further disseminating available information by retweeting other users' messages' (Bruns, 2012, p. 4, 2018). Bruns here sees journalists' role as complementary, where they can facilitate and curate the processes of news dissemination and discussion by also driving reader traffic to their own (or their employers') websites. In this role, journalists are not necessarily breaking new stories, but they continue to track existing news events and contribute with new critical perspectives on issues (Bruns, 2021, p. 252).

Another aspect of news gathering that is judged to be positive specifically concerns political reporting. The ubiquitous presence of both political and media actors in the platform has also affected their relationship. The increased pace of political cycles and political communication processes, as well as political actors' direct broadcasting of information to their audiences, creates a feeling of closeness that also translates to a proximity to power (Molyneux & McGregor, 2021). In practice, this translates to much more efficient access to leaders and those holding power. With reference to the U.S. context, Molyneux and McGregor (2021, p. 5) note that 'following Obama's use of Twitter as the first "social media president", tweets practically replaced press briefings in the Trump administration', pointing to

Twitter as the primary source to encounter and interact with elected officials.

Another positive side-effect of news gathering occurring on Twitter is 'the orientation towards more transparency' (Hedman & Djerf-Pierre, 2013, p. 371) as journalistic processes are now more visible. Revers (2014, p. 823) rightly argues that the push for transparency does not rely on the employment of technologies themselves, but on the cultural shifts the technological developments enable. The author refers to 'growing insistence on disclosure of information and openness of procedures' which 'mutually reinforce each other' (2014, p. 823). Indeed, the shift on changing some of the professional norms, such as transparency, to abide to the cultural shifts occurring due to technologies like Twitter, is already implied by the changing nature of the audience noted above.

1.1.3.3 Tweets as a news source

Apart from benefiting the process of newsgathering, Twitter in itself often becomes the 'news source' with users' tweets being embedded in journalists' online or offline journalistic products. For example, Broersma and Graham (2012) refer to several functions that tweets have in newspaper reporting and coverage. They are used: to 'add flavour to a story' by offering background information; to illustrate an argument, trend, or opinion that is presented in the article; to indicate public sentiment about political actors; to trigger news coverage (for example, in the case of an offensive tweet); as a means of adding politicians' views on a topic especially when those politicians are not accessible otherwise; and to entertain their readers (for instance, in the case of humorous or funny tweets) (Broersma & Graham, 2012, 2013; Oschatz et al., 2021).

Over the years, and during Twitter's evolution, the phenomenon of fully quoting tweets became a more conscious choice that led to the extensive use of tweets in legacy news coverage (von Nordheim et al., 2018). Molyneux and McGregor (2021, p. 2) discuss this process in terms of Twitter's impact on news making and argue that

> journalists have come to treat tweets more like content, an interchangeable building block of news, than like sources, whose ideas and messages must be subject to scrutiny and verification. Sources are interrogated; content, on the other hand, is simply reproduced.

Their research shows that tweets are considered newsworthy, even to the extent that they are the 'new *vox populi*' (McGregor & Molyneux,

2020: 601). Whether or not this is the case, or whether it makes a news story more dynamic (Papacharissi, 2015, p. 31), what can be said with some certainty is that Twitter is now a recognised and very frequently used source for news.

1.1.3.4 The personal touch

Another element that has been evaluated positively in terms of Twitter's impact on news journalism concerns the blurring boundaries between the personal and the professional. Increasingly, it has become an orthodoxy that news journalists must be seen to be something more than in their professional roles: they must now be seen to be both more friendly and approachable as well solicitous of other people's views. And while this comes as a challenge to journalists, it is the case that many are now expected to use social media in a way that 'opens up their personal self a little bit' because it can 'make them [journalists] look authentic, friendly, and transparent' (Lee, 2020, p. 2098). In addition, it has been argued that the increasingly personalised or opinionated use of social media may add to journalists' trustworthiness, likability and credibility (Johnson, 2020; Lee, 2015). As Lee also suggests, there is a positive relationship between self-disclosure and perceptions of attitudes towards journalists' work. Interestingly, Lee (2020, p. 2108) also notes that 'the negative influence of hurting objectivity is not large enough to offset the positive effect of self-disclosure'.

Being perceived to be more publicly accessible allows journalists to interact directly with audiences, to engage in conversations and to add their endorsement on stories' views. According to Molyneux's study (2015, p. 930), journalists 'appreciate Twitter as an outlet that lets them do what they feel they cannot in a traditional news environment', for example to express humorous opinions about political processes. Even journalists who are more 'old school' in their professional outlook are increasingly more intimate with their audience and are aware of the development of their own personal brand (Molyneux, 2015, p. 12). Whether or not the personal touch increases trust or represents a departure from objectivity that in some way undermines trust, is still an open question, with editors and journalists remaining cautious about engaging personally to avoid undermining trust (Newman, 2022).

1.1.3.5 Branding the self

Ottovordemgentschefelde (2017, p. 76) refers to Twitter profiles as being journalists' digital business cards or portfolios that 'establish competitive superiority'. These discussions about the development of a personal brand for journalists on Twitter have intensified over years with some scholars seeing personal branding as key to building a career in journalism (Bech Sillesen, 2015; Brems et al., 2016; Hedman, 2016; Molyneux et al., 2018). Building a brand presumably entails journalists branding themselves 'as a way of self-commodification that seeks to increase their market value' (Mellado & Hermida, 2021, p. 4). Since 2013, there have been many studies looking at Twitter's impact on journalists' market value. Hedman and Djerf-Pierre (2013, p. 372), for example, suggest that Twitter enhances 'the individual's social capital in the professional field, at least in the eyes of other active social media users'. According to Barthel et al. (2015, p. 2), this means that Twitter provides 'an ideal platform to gain visibility, credibility and prestige' which could potentially be transferrable to the offline world (Jukes, 2019). The conceptualisation of professional branding in terms of social capital takes into account the size of one's network (as in the number of followers and follows) and other activity metrics that allow showcasing the strength of one's status via interactions and platform metrics (Hedman, 2020; Swasy 2016). When personal branding is seen as a form of 'accumulation of social capital' (Simon, 2019), Twitter can play a critical role in the legitimation of journalists within or outside the platform.

In essence, the branding of the self is journalists' attempt 'to commodify their online persona' and 'to tie their audience to themselves rather than their employees' (Maares et al., 2020, p. 4). Such branding is also an attempt to establish a particular journalist as trustworthy. In short, they become a form of news brand which is measured by their personal following on social media platforms. This form of 'personal news brand' is detached from that of their employers to the extent that it can be transferred if they move to another employer. Bruns (2021, p. 257) underlines that this is particularly important for new journalists entering the profession, for whom 'especially at a time of continuing economic stress, such entrepreneurial thinking is now a requirement'. Lieberman (2021) confirms this finding, by adding that many journalists credit their professional accomplishments to relationships they first cultivated on Twitter.

Overall, personal branding is judged in terms of how successfully it identifies a particular journalistic persona and a personal digital portfolio which is not always strictly associated with the organisations they work for. In a nutshell, it is a form of acquiring career advantage (Bech Sillesen, 2015). The only question that remains unanswered is whether personal branding actually raises questions over 'the place and purpose of the institution of journalism' (Molyneux et al., 2018, p. 1399).

1.2 Twitter as distorting news journalism

Platforms like Twitter are central to the discursive character of political and civil life. Moore (2018, p. 6) is correct to note that Twitter is complicit in 'restructuring our politics, undermining existing institutions and remaking the role of the citizen'. What follows below is a set of specific concerns that justify this overarching complaint. The fact that our political and communication systems have become faster and more virtual does not in and of itself explain the deleterious effects that are attributed to Twitter's contribution to contemporary society in general and with news journalism in particular. In his book *The Twittering Machine*, Seymour (2019, p. 29) describes the process of the inversion that occurred in cyber-idealism and turned it into cyber-cynicism – how anonymity, creative autonomy and space for multitudes to express themselves turned into trolling, 'fake news' and lynch mobs, respectively. While this is not the whole story (as the above has tried to show), it is depressingly a large chunk of the story. What follows is a list of well-documented concerns that focus on the cost to news journalism in and through its relationship and attachment to Twitter and how ultimately traditional standards clash with perceived new possibilities. As noted above, there are three basic arguments that support the view that Twitter distorts and represents a cost to news journalism: (a) Twitter causes irreconcilable professional pressures; (b) Twitter underpins information disorder; and (c) Twitter is ideally suited to mediate populism and the coarsening of political and civil discourse and devalues journalism.

1.2.1 Twitter's effect on professional pressures

Twitter introduced speed and immediacy to news, which served the purpose of providing audiences immediately with informed breaking news. The problem being to what extent does this form of instant news need to be checked and researched and to what extent could it be taken at face value given certain caveats. Accuracy is simply a question of 'getting it right' which for the news journalists means through 'an effective investigation of contemporary events' (Harrison, 2019a). Here the key point is what constitutes an 'effective investigation.' It is not surprising that some studies point to this 'constant tension' between speed and accuracy and between efficiency and quality (Gulyas, 2013; Lasorsa et al., 2012; Messner et al., 2011). How to reconcile these conflicting demands has according to Min and Fink (2021, p. 6) produced a situation where news journalists are now in need of constant technological 're-skilling' and 'up-skilling' to meet those demands. Messner et al. (2011, p. 7) refer to time constraints that led many news organisations 'to treat their Twitter accounts like an automated RSS feed with little audience interaction'. In Greece, it was found that the immediacy and speed of Twitter required that in some news organisations and amongst some news journalists that they redistributed previously published content automatically (Dagoula, 2012; 2019). Having to produce their journalistic output faster but also 'to rely on unverified information that has been posted by questionable sources, or to react to trending stories that might not have much relevance beyond a small group of online users' represent new pressures on news journalism which threaten to undermine the traditional journalistic norm of accuracy (Willnat & Weaver, 2018, p. 891). Hedman (2020, p. 672) suggests that the selection and presentation of the content occurred with the aim of 'achieving maximal attention' and this relies on two aspects: (a) the logic of virality and (b) the importance of one's networks and metrics. Simplistically, this relies on the principle of 'the higher the numbers, the higher the status' (Hedman, 2020, p. 672).

When journalists themselves spoke about challenges and tensions related to the growing use of Twitter, they pointed out that one result of editorial directives was 'to constantly "match" what competitors were doing with regard to the use of their Twitter feeds'. The general criticism directed at Twitter was 'for enabling constraints on their ability to exercise control over the news agenda', as shown by Chadha and Wells (2016, p. 1031). In other words, journalists interviewed in this study saw their professional remit as one of increasingly having to follow the 'Twitter agenda' (Chadha & Wells, 2016). Failure to do so, it was feared, would mean that those news organisations which ignored the Twitter agenda would risk placing themselves at a competitive and commercial disadvantage in the news sector. On this occasion, the lack of use of Twitter would result in a form of negative branding both at organisational and at individual level. Jukes (2019, p. 255) confirms this view of the pressure journalists felt to post on Twitter. One of his interviewees connected this pressure with the 'increasing expectations that he and his colleagues should promote themselves and encourage followers to click through to underlying stories'. In a similar vein, Barnard (2016, p. 191) uses as an example the 'famous proclamation' uttered by BBC News Global News Director Peter Horrocks 'tweet or be sacked', which according to Horrocks aimed 'to impress upon them [BBC journalists] that the use of social media was no longer discretionary for BBC journalists' (Miller, 2011).

Popularity which is quantified in metrics constitutes 'a critical benchmark for journalists and news organisations alike, allowing them to make assumptions about their own performance and impact' (Simon, 2019, p. 1200). Here we should not underestimate the addictive aspect this might create. 'In curating the self, notifications (which could be seen as a form of clickbait) light up the "reward centres" of the brain, so we feel bad if the metrics we accumulate on our different platforms do not express enough approval', writes Seymour (2019, p. 31): especially when our work performance is evaluated on that basis. Indeed, metrics have become one way to evaluate journalistic performance and to accordingly evaluate their position in terms of prestige and their social capital. Scholars, for example, have linked journalists' Twitter presence with the accumulation of social capital. Usher et al. (2018, p. 327) note that 'Twitter plays a critical role in the legitimation of journalists and is, thus, a habitus-defining form of social capital'. Simplified, with reference to political journalists in Washington, they argue that 'Twitter may well be what makes or breaks a journalist in Washington'. Twitter metrics do not officially inform hiring decisions or promotions, but they can play an implicit role for executives in news organisations (Kueng, 2017, as cited in Simon, 2019, p. 1212). However, this datafication is deeply ingrained in newsrooms (van Dijck et al., 2018, p. 58). Van Dijck et al. (2018, p. 53) explain metrics through datafication, which is prescribed in platforms as a key mechanism, and suggests that every form of user interaction can be captured as data. User metrics have become vital to the news process, primarily because news organisations organise some of their practices, like their production and distribution of news, around platform data (van Dijck et al., 2018, p. 71).

Naturally, this puts pressure on journalists to perform and to consistently prove that they can add value to the organisation they are working for (Hanusch & Bruns, 2017). The pressure to perform and to 'deliver' in terms of metrics has an overwhelming effect. This is added to the already existing (and predetermined by Twitter's design) pressure concerning an overwhelming amount of information. Barnidge et al. (2020) point to studies that exemplify many journalists' fatigue with public engagement on Twitter, whereas Lawrence's (2015, p. 101) interviews with political journalists reveal that there are reporters that 'simply step out of the Twitter flow from time to time, returning to their pre-social-media routines and crossing their fingers that nothing important happens that they risk missing' and a few reporters that 'actively disengage from Twitter while they are trying to file a story or report an event because they find it distracting'. Similar results are provided by Lieberman (2021) who identified a small but a growing group of prominent journalists who either disconnected or dramatically scaled back their use of Twitter, either by deleting previous tweets, imposing a ban on new ones, or deactivating their accounts. Interestingly, even journalists that left Twitter had something positive to say about Twitter's contribution to journalism and mentioned that their disconnection was not necessarily permanent (Kale 2021; Lieberman, 2021). Overall, though, the overreliance on new tools, such as Twitter, can be seen as a cause for mental and physical burnout for journalists (Bossio and Nelson, 2021, p. 1377).

Adding to the particular pressures on journalists is that they now find themselves in the position of having to imagine who their audience is based on how they sounded in tweets and the nature and tone of their response. Both constant follows and 'issue-led' occasional engagers provide diverse responses to issues. Audiences are anything but consistent in what they say or what they are concerned about. The idea of a journalist (or editor) knowing their audience ('our readers want to know') is fractured and fragmented and relies on metrics that have probability of error in depicting what an audience believes. What both editor and journalist are forced to do is to constantly anticipate approval and this represents a form of self-censorship.

The problem of the imagined new audience is straightforward and not new – journalists have always been addressing their work to a preconceived version of the reader or listener. The problem is that the idea of concurrent multiple audiences defies marketing and processes of accurately identifying their news requirements. Even assuming that their primary audience is other people on Twitter is essentially wrong as their potential audiences can increase exponentially (Lieberman, 2021). The importance of a journalist's imagined audience lies with the substantial influence it has on the choices news journalists make such as the subjects they select to reporting on and the ways they tell their stories (Robinson, 2019). Presuming that 'the potential audience for anything posted on the internet is the entire internet', this produces a strong pressure towards conformity with the values and mores of one's (perceived or imagined) peers (Seymour, 2019, p. 39). Targeting specific audience members exacerbates the problem by setting limits on the size, scope and particulars of the audience by a process of talking only to some interests. Finally, this process of managing, monitoring and responding to feedback, to be aware of others' actions and to interpret their audiences' interests (Marwick & boyd, 2010, p. 130) might also lead to the point of considering self-censoring so as to avoid unwanted reactions from the Twitter community. Seymour (2019, p. 39) writes that the only way to conform successfully is by being 'unutterably bland and platitudinous' – in other words, by self-censoring anything that might be considered controversial. Moreover, this is no guarantee that one can avoid being a fitting target for abuse. Journalists now must constantly re-evaluate their understanding of their audiences. Twitter has brought into existence 'concurrent multiple audiences' with whom they could interact directly. These 'imagined' audiences are typically ultimately idealised as stereotypical social constructs with diverse news requirements. Such stereotypes span for example: (a) concerned citizens with a need to know; (b) consumers of a certain kind of news products; (c) groups dogmatically clinging to fixed partisan views which needed sustaining; and (d) ephemeral audiences who are capable of being influenced and led (Harrison, 2019a). These news requirements needed to be constantly anticipated which means the return of a traditional disconnect between the followed and the followers (Marwick & boyd, 2010, p. 117). In a nutshell, journalists now need to target tweets or conceal and reveal information based on who they imagine is listening reading or interacting in some other way (Marwick & boyd, 2010, p. 130).

1.2.2 Twitter as underpinning information disorder

One of the main concerns about Twitter has to do with the ways it accommodates information disorder thereby making the job of news journalism even more difficult when it comes to the issue of accuracy (see above) and the homologous character of news that seek to represent events as they are. According to Wardle and Derakhsan (2017), information disorder is an inclusive term that describes the sharing of false information which comprises disinformation, misinformation and mal-information. Respectively, disinformation consists of information that is false and deliberately created to harm a person, social group, organisation or country. Misinformation consists of information that is false, but not created with the intention of causing harm, while mal-information consists of information that is based on reality, used to inflict harm on a person, organisation or country. Adding to the lexica of information disorder is the phrase 'fake news' which refers to 'information that has been deliberately fabricated and disseminated with the intention to deceive and mislead others into believing falsehoods or doubting verifiable facts' (McGonagle, 2017, p. 203). In essence, information disorder comprises an environment that spans 'playful hoaxes to belligerent propaganda or incitement to violence' (McGonagle, 2017, p. 204). However, it is described that contemporary information disorder essentially requires a troll culture in and through which 'alternative realities' are expressed (Rauch, 2021, p. 13).

The problem of information disorder for news journalism is not new – Schudson and Zelizer (2017, p. 1) note that there has been 'a long history of journalistic hoaxes, scandals, lies, satire and exaggerations' that dates back hundreds of years to the invention of the print. However, the participatory elements of new platforms (such as Twitter) have made it easy for a wide range of actors to create sophisticated content on a large scale and to disseminate it very quickly thereby compounding the problems for news journalism with regard to what should be reported as accurate and what counts as homologous news. According to Schudson and Zelizer (2017, p. 3), this issue has caused a blurring of 'the borders between professional journalists and others who through digital media have easy access to promoting their ideas, perspectives, factual reports, pranks, inanities, conspiracy theories, fakes and lies'. Hermida (2010, pp. 299–300) cites the concern expressed by news journalists 'that many of the messages on Twitter amount to unsubstantiated rumours and wild inaccuracies which are raised when there is a major breaking news event'. One journalist is reported to have said that 'it's like searching for medical advice in an online world of quacks and cures'. A problem exacerbated by what Higgins (2017, p. 4) refers to as 'a combination of the democratisation of information media production and the de-professionalisation of formal news gathering' and what (Wardle, 2017) refers to as the problems associated with a participatory information ecosystem accompanied by a conscious disaffection with conventional authority. The dilemma for the journalist in reductionist, straightforward and helpful terms is either 'tweet first, verify later' or 'verify first and publish later' (Bruno, 2011).

Inevitably, well-meaning attempts by news journalism to manage information disorder have in some cases made the problem worse. Consider the case of the new participatory audience who were encouraged by news organisations to support the co-creation of content, collaborative filtering and curating of news content. The principle being to ensure conformity to professional standards and to ensure the audience 'stayed with you' both as producer and as consumer (Papacharissi, 2014, p. 34). And while this might sound admirable, the result was that this shift in news sourcing simply meant that tweets were suddenly treated as content to be simply reproduced rather than as sources which required verification (Molyneux & McGregor 2021,

p. 2). A shift that confirms Rauch's (2021, p. 13) view that 'digital media have turned out to be better attuned to outrage and disinformation than to conversation and knowledge' which also ensured that 'emotional, partisan news content is disproportionately amplified in social media' (Hassel, 2020, p. 2).[1]

Adding to information disorder is the problem of balance and representation – an impartial assessment of competing views – where the problem is that Twitter has become an increasingly integral element of new media information cycles (Nielsen & Schroder, 2014). In principle, the new networked audience can (as noted above) participate in these cycles and have their views and opinions represented and, in principle, communicate directly with the speaker (Marwick & boyd, 2010). The suggestion here is that ordinary users (or alternatively, non-elites) are able to affect news production through 'timely interventions and sometimes direct, one-to-one, micro-level interactions with professional journalists' by also affecting 'the meaning and flow of information' (Chadwick, 2013, p. 89).

However, even early studies reveal that when it comes to 'elite users', which includes media and journalists, their attention and communication is highly 'homophilous' (a sociological term that refers to the tendency of individuals to associate and bond with similar others). As Wu et al. (2011, p. 9) express it, 'with celebrities following celebrities, media following media, and bloggers following bloggers' – a tendency that is confirmed by recent studies (Molyneux et al., 2018; Molyneux & Mourão, 2019). For example, Molyneux and Mourão (2019, p. 261) note that 'reporters tend to interact with each other much more than with anyone outside the profession' and this subsequently defines their forms of interaction which entails frequent use of retweets to promote their co-workers, use of quote tweets to comment on the work of their peers at other news organisations and replies mostly to their inner circle. Likewise, Barnidge et al. (2020, p. 418) find that 'it is the "usual suspects" who are most likely to engage journalists in these spaces, which means that Twitter is more "business as usual" than it is a new connection point for journalists'. This echoes previous research on Twitter and U.K. journalists' accounts (Dagoula, 2017). In sum, there is an overly reliance on a non-representative few with vested interests in having have their views represented. A return in fact to traditional ways of doing news journalism. Representation and balance are not products of new Twitter-based news cycles. Even so, these findings contradict the idea that journalists engage with diverse new audience members by supporting the idea that existing networks and hierarchies are still a focal point of Twitter-based news journalism.

Imbalance also includes the case of gender bias. For example, various studies (Maares et al., 2020, p. 2; McGregor & Molyneux, 2020; Usher et al., 2018) found that gendered echo chambers still remain. Usher et al.'s (2018, p. 327) study of Washington's political journalists found significant indicators of gender bias and suggest that on Twitter 'political journalism is deeply insular and self-involved, much like it is offline'. This intra-elite discourse clearly affects their perception of other social realities, as well as their news-sourcing practices. Similarly, Johnson et al. (2018, p. 869) in their research on economic journalists in Belgium found no fundamental changes in the news production process as 'Twitter is implemented within existing sourcing practices' with 'traditional elite sources remaining omnipresent' in both online and offline source networks 'with only a very small group of active Twitter users including more bottom-up sources in their online networks'. Equally, von Nordheim et al.'s (2018, p. 821) ten-year study on *The New York Times*, *The Guardian* and *Süddeutsche Zeitung* show that 'the use of non-elite voices from Twitter has not increased considerably in any of the newspapers. The general increase in sourcing Twitter is obviously primarily due to an increase in elite sources'. Freedman (2016, as cited in Curran et al., p. 101) also challenges the view that digital networks have shifted power from 'the centre to the periphery and from elites to ordinary users and creators' by privileging 'accumulation strategies that are designed to reward corporate interests more than to empower individual actors'.

All of the above points directly contradict the common assumption that Twitter helps to enrich news sourcing and to enhance journalists' engagement with audiences, in so far as their reach and popularity seems to be shaped through their interaction with specific, mostly elite, accounts. It is as if legacy media has colonised Twitter in the same way that legacy media colonised the news segment of cyberspace (Curran et al., 2016, p. 23).

1.2.3 Twitter, mediated populism and the coarsening of political and civil discourse: a toxic environment

This section began with Moore's (2018) observation that 'Twitter has contributed to restructuring our politics, undermining existing institutions and remaking the role of the citizen' and it has done this in and through its relationship with news journalism. To be specific it has done this in the role it has played as a tool for the dissemination of partisan news. Though to be clear Twitter did not create partisan news. Rather, the concern here is how Twitter plays a significant role in contributing to such tendency.

Combined with information disorder, mediated populism thrives on polarisation (Osmuden et al., 2021) disseminated through the many channels of partisan news. Its core features consist of, through Müller's lens (2016, p. 19), a 'particular moralistic imagination of politics, a way of perceiving the political world that sets a morally pure and fully unified (but ultimately fictional) people against elites who are deemed corrupt or in some other way morally inferior'. Populism is regarded as being anti-elitist and anti-pluralist. The relationship between populism and Twitter here is interesting about the way it also seeks to undercut news journalism by providing a tool for politicians to address their audiences directly. Urbinati (2019) notes that populism always configures itself into a new form of direct representation of the people, one that acquires the rhetoric of being democratic and truly inclusive of those who are exclusively defined as *the* people. One means by which it does this is as Müller (2016, p. 35) notes, by wanting to cut out the middleman, whether this be traditional parties and party organisations that act as intermediaries between citizens and politicians, or journalists.

According to populist politicians what the 'mainstream' news media do is to distort political reality by excluding the interest of the 'real people' or 'silent majority'. They fail to represent the 'real people' serving only their own interests and the interests of hidden elite power and accordingly they use media on behalf of the elite to the detriment of the 'real people'. What Twitter does in this case is to allow populist politicians or leaders to speak directly to the real people and on occasions to skim the process of mediation and to shape the news agenda, by ignoring traditional journalism (Higgins, 2017). Cowls and Schroeder (2018, pp. 151–152) refer to 'a populist undercurrent in American politics' that existed for a long time and which has now 'propelled via Twitter, which bypassed the gatekeepers of traditional media'. This way 'populism could emerge interstitially to win out over the ideological and organizational stranglehold of the two parties'. Added to which Manucci (2017, p. 10) clearly summarises how social media facilitate populistic processes by being 'a perfect channel for the diffusion of populist messages':

> first, populist actors often accuse the traditional media system of being controlled by the mainstream political elites, and therefore they consider the new social media as the only neutral and independent arena; second, populist actors build their credibility on their links with ordinary people and advocate unrestricted popular sovereignty, hence the possibility of communicating directly with their electorate can reinforce their image of being

approachable people; third, social media are more informal and favour a type of communication close to colloquial language, based on emotions rather than on reasoning, this being close to a populist discursive style.

To this end, Twitter feeds and sustains a specific type of political mediated discourse, one which favours antagonism, and not agonism, by adopting a coarse form of discourse that is 'obsessive, feverish and zero-sum' and that contributes to 'an environment that breeds, at best, suspicion and hostility to opposing worldviews and, at worst, festering radicalisation' (Lothian-McLean, 2022). For instance, commenting on Trump's antagonistic use of Twitter, Cowls and Schroeder (2018) note that he used it 'in three stages to attack his enemies: first, taking aim at his primary opponents; then, with the race reduced to two, his Democratic opponent; and since the election, his new main enemy, the media'. Twitter is a format for one-way dissemination over debate, as the carrier of short, non-cohesive declarations (Higgins, 2017) which undercuts and attacks the traditional values of news journalism. For Higgins (2017), Twitter is the ideal platform for appealing to any supposed 'silent majority' as it is a completely democratic, open-access, cost-free platform that in principle has no restrictions and no filtering (apart from rare, extreme cases) and that allows a political candidate 'to appeal at a personal level to anyone who is against anything and make him or her feel like part of a vast shared community without having to meet or even acknowledge any of its other members'. Essentially, Twitter facilitates the processes of oversimplifying and transforming political messages into slogans.

An important point now is that mediated populism by Twitter plays a role in ensuring that the information disorder noted above is tuned into a toxic news environment based on antagonism of an unforgiving kind. Twitter's role was to some extent endorsed by the complicity of some of the mainstream news media whose news journalism was undermined by Twitter. A complicity driven by the commercial pressures associated with audience share and correspondingly increased revenues. Cowls and Schroeder (2018, p. 154) refer to several senior TV executives in the United States who noted that ratings increased as they made stories out of Trump's tweets which they constantly reproduced in the news. Adding to this was the fact that these tweets also sent followers to his preferred news sites and to reject news stories (as fake news) from other news organisation. To this end, the authors suggest that Trump was 'able to set the agenda by tweeting positions that were guaranteed a wide audience in mainstream media' (Cowls & Schroeder, 2018, p. 154).

Mediated populism is not the only element of a toxic information disorder in which Twitter played a role. Toxicity also entails a facilitation of abuse of journalists. In 2018, Amnesty International published an extensive research report called 'Toxic Twitter' which revealed the extent of online abuse of women users within the platform (*Amnesty International*, 2018). The report's results paint a worrying picture of how Twitter can be a toxic place for its female users. From its analysis of hundreds of thousands of tweets sent in 2017 Amnesty found that female journalists and politicians were subjected to some kind of harassment or abuse on the social network roughly every 30 seconds. According to Amnesty International (2018), this abusive experience has a 'detrimental effect' on women's 'right to express themselves equally, freely and without fear' leading them to self-censoring, to limiting their interactions, and to even signing-off the platform entirely.

Following this, a recent UNESCO (2020) report found that 73% of 625 women journalist respondents from 125 countries confirmed that they had experienced online violence, namely misogynistic harassment and abuse, orchestrated disinformation campaigns that exploit misogynistic narratives, and digital privacy and security threats that increase physical risks associated with online violence (Posetti et al., 2020). Interestingly, 'even in supposedly "safe" places of the developed world that have historically prized press freedom', news media – and consequently journalists – are considered a target (Lewis et al., 2020, p. 1048). The phenomenon of online harassment and abuse is not recent, and it is not just gendered. In 2016, Warzel published on *Buzzfeed News* an extensive article on 'Twitter's 10-Year Failure to Stop Harassment' taking a longitudinal approach to the issue. Indeed, 'for years Twitter had been criticized for allowing a culture of harassment to fester largely unchecked on its service' (Gillespie, 2018, p. 24), particularly in terms of developing the infrastructure, the procedural and technical mechanisms, to respond. Even though the phenomenon is not new – it is 'as old as the Internet itself' (Lewis et al., 2020, p. 1049) – Lewis et al. (2020, p. 1049) note that 'online harassment appears to have become considerably more widespread on social media platforms'. Similarly, Bouvier and Rosenbaum (2020, pp. 317–319) emphasise how Twitter allows for conversations that are 'dark, degrading, and dehumanizing' with arguments rarely moving beyond incivility and where disagreement with another's views can swiftly turn into an exchange of abusive accusations and insults.

28 *The two dominant views of Twitter and news journalism*

What emerges from seeing Twitter as somehow enabling journalism and/or as somehow distorting news journalism are a series of claims that centre on a combination of both analytical and empirical work. I now wish to examine these claims by considering the findings of a longitudinal study which had two elements. First, a qualitative study which consisted of research interviews with news journalists that explored what they said about their uses of Twitter and, second, by subsequently analysing how these journalists' Twitter accounts changed across the period of 2009–2021. To do this requires that this study is framed explicitly in terms of its methodological assumption. Here by adopting (for reasons given in the introduction) the evolutionary approach known as punctuated equilibrium which consists of three fundamental evolutionary stages disruption, adaption and normalisation. It is these three stages, I wish to analyse next in terms of their usefulness for understanding the relationship between Twitter and changes to the institution of news journalism attributed to the impact of Twitter.

Note

1 Twitter itself recognises the gravity of the problem. In a recent update of its safety policy, it also introduced a 'crisis misinformation policy' (Roth, 2022). Roth, Twitter's head of Safety and Integrity, necessitates this global policy as a way

> to guide our efforts to elevate credible, authoritative information, and will help to ensure viral misinformation isn't amplified or recommended by us during crises. In times of crisis, misleading information can undermine public trust and cause further harm to already vulnerable communities. Alongside our existing work to make reliable information more accessible during crisis events, this new approach will help to slow the spread by us of the most visible, misleading content, particularly that which could lead to severe harms.

2 Punctuated equilibrium
Disruption, adaption and normalisation

2.1 The institution of news journalism and punctuated equilibrium

Probably the best definition of an institution was provided by Smelser (1997). He argues that an institution comprises of 'those complexes of roles, normative systems and legitimising values that constitute a functionally defined set of activities that gain permanence through the very process of institutionalisation' (Smelser, 1997, p. 46). Using this definition, Harrison and Pukallus (2022) note how the institution of news journalism is organised around attempts to socialise news journalists into ways of undertaking their role, how these ways reflect what a particular news organisation requires of its news journalists, and what is institutionally acceptable. In such manner, the norms of journalism circumscribe the practical and ethical basis for doing news journalism. Such norms are subject to pressures brought about by social change. For example, Kreiss (2016, p. 73) points out that ideally, on normative grounds, the institution of journalism provides the public infrastructure of the civil sphere; the master forums within which many forms of civic monitoring take place and access wider publics; and the grounding in the universalistic democratic criteria through which scepticism occurs in the public interest. Additionally, Kreiss (2016, p. 73) notes that 'it is the moral and civic orientation of journalism that grounds its value as an institution (...)'. This is linked to the perception of journalism as a civic institution. Drawing on Alexander (2016, p. 10) we need to highlight that journalism encompasses professional ethics and civic morals and consequently its functions extend much further than just the publicising and networking of information (2016, p. 12). Of course, the settings for these ethics and civil morals only have force if they are institutionalised and manifest in news

DOI: 10.4324/9781003231776-3

organisations. Changes to them are always challenges to traditionally held norms and standards. To understand this, we must return to the processes of social change and their impact upon institutions and their constituent organisations. Moore (1963) in his classic account of social change[1] argues that it could consist of: (a) major shifts of revolutionary kind, and (b) steady evolutionary development.[2] The question emerging here is which kind of process of social change is the institution of news journalism subject to with the introduction of Twitter into ways of producing and disseminating news: revolutionary or evolutionary? As noted in the introduction, the former (revolutionary process of social change) entails change generated through crisis or 'black swan' moments (Taleb, 2007) – in other words, fundamental changes in practices which are unexpected, sudden and drastic. In those terms, social change could be considered as consisting of moments of 'shock', and subsequent adjustments which replace traditional modes of practice. The latter (evolutionary process of social change) entails understanding the gradual transformation of institutions through a series of stages of increasing complexity and differentiation.

To judge whether an institution (such as news journalism that is defined by a particular set of rules, norms and principles) has been subject to revolutionary or evolutionary change, it is necessary to examine how stable it is. According to Parsons (1971), an institution defines the general conditions of stability of a social system, by being understood as a set of rules, norms and principles.[3] Clearly, the modern institution of news journalism (as I shall show in Chapters 3 and 4[4]) is not in an unstable condition, but rather remains attached to a continuous set of civil rules, norms and principles (Harrison, 2019a). In short, it is subject to evolutionary processes. This is not to say that the institution of news journalism is not subject to crisis of one kind or another (Alexander, 2016). Nor is it to suggest that the corporate structures of news organisations are not subject to economic vicissitudes, or that news organisations see news journalism in some ossified way. Nor that communication technology has no impact. But rather, it is to suggest that such changes that occur in the institution of news journalism, occur in an evolutionary manner. Besides, according to Moore (1963, p. 13), stability can also entail flexibility that provides the possibility for innovation. This is because institutional evolutionary social change is directly connected to social outcomes. In relation to our understanding of the social outcomes of technological change for news journalism, the theory of punctuated equilibrium allows us to understand institutional change in news journalism without succumbing to technological determinism: a view which suggests that social

Punctuated equilibrium: disruption, adaption and normalisation

change is teleological and somehow pre-ordained by the nature of the technology. As Alexander (2016, p. 23) argues, neither technology nor (for that matter) economics exercise their social effects in isolation, but are mediated by the professional ethics of journalism and the civic morals that anchor them. Alexander (2016, p. 9) links technological determinism to a theoretical reductionism that sees journalism as being merely informational and notes that 'such reduction of news to information lends support to the fatalistic picture of journalism's displacement'.

The problem with prioritising technological change consists in the following charges. Innovation is linked to promise and expectations that new technologies, actors and practices might be the solution to contemporary journalistic problems (Bossio & Nelson, 2021, p. 1377). Digital technology is presented as sustaining journalism (Luengo, 2021, p. vi), technology is seen as rescuing journalism from its perpetual crisis (Min & Fink, 2021, p. 4); and technology becomes disassociated from the rhythms of everyday life. Curran et al. (2016, p. 9) make the following observations about the Internet. The central weakness of optimistic perspectives (in relation to the Internet), he argues, is that they are based on inference rather than evidence and therefore fail to recognise that the impact of technology is filtered through the structures and processes of society. By adopting an evolutionary theory conceived of in terms of a process of punctuated equilibrium, we avoid these charges.

In essence, punctuated equilibrium is a process which consists of three stages: short-term disruption, short-term adaption, and medium- and long-term normalisation. Vollmer (2013, p. 14) claims that evolutionary theory encourages us to incorporate analyses of how disruptions initially take place as well as investigations of how they subsequently spread, escalate, or die down, and how different manifestations of order are possibly involved in this, within a single analytical perspective on the longitudinal development of order. What this means is that institutional change is not best understood as a revolutionary process, as if something new or dramatic or innovative causes wholesale and systemic change to the way we value and understand something, the norms associated with, and how we do things. Rather, change is typically a steady state and normal and is mainly driven by the increasing complexity of the social system and the separation of functions/responsibility brought about by this complexity. Occasionally, change takes the form of adjustments made to the social system brought about by social movements.

Punctuated equilibrium explains both gradual and abrupt change in the context of a single theory – change is regarded as a punctuation/

interruption in a relatively stable state (Vollmer, 2013). The theory not only summarises the processes of disruption, adaption and normalisation, but also unlocks the scale of each stage. Additionally, as Alexander et al. (2008, p. 558) state, social and institutional change is best conceived as 'a gradual transformation through a series of stages'. They also point out that human history consists of a series of stages of complexity rather than single moments of radical transformations – this is also evidenced by Toffler's[5] great waves (agricultural age, industrial age, information age) and even more so by the fact that there is not a clear-cut transition between the waves, as some features of the older exist alongside with the new. Possibly 'an accumulation of changes may eventually result in transformation that amounts to a revolution' (Alexander et al., 2008, p. 558), but arguably, this would still require a tectonic shift. And in our case, Twitter is not seen as or conceived of in tectonic or revolutionary terms. Alexander (2016, p. 3) puts the matter this way:

> because social change is endemic in modern societies, it is hardly surprising that the history of journalism has been marked by continuous eruptions of crisis. Just as current anxieties have been triggered by computerization and digital news, so were earlier crises of journalism linked to technological shifts that demanded new forms of economic organization.

In the history of journalism what can be discerned is its constant evolution via the constant introduction of new technologies each of which marks what Alexander (2016) calls the 'continuous eruption of crisis'. Indeed, Alexander goes so far as to argue that news journalists experience their institutional independence as continuously fragile and threatened adding that 'even as they successfully defend their professional ethics, journalists experience them as vulnerable to subversion in the face of technological and economic change' (2016, p. 3). For Luengo (2002, p. vii), crises are the driving force for changes to news journalism.

The argument here is that each crisis follows a pattern of short-term disruption caused by the crisis (stability is punctuated) which necessitates short-term adaption as the crisis is managed and tactically adjusted to, followed by medium- and long-term normalisation as the crisis is stabilised and change accepted as a new way of understanding or doing something (Figure 2.1).

It is punctuated equilibrium that provides us with the best way to evaluate institutional change. It shows how elements of dramatic

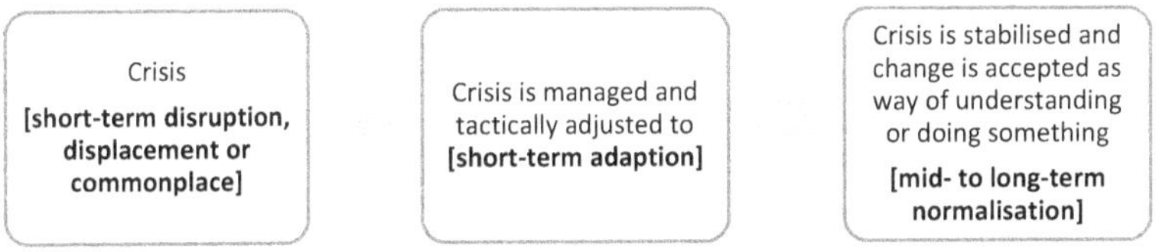

Punctuated equilibrium: disruption, adaption and normalisation

> Crisis
> [short-term disruption, displacement or commonplace]

> Crisis is managed and tactically adjusted to [short-term adaption]

> Crisis is stabilised and change is accepted as way of understanding or doing something [mid- to long-term normalisation]

Figure 2.1 Main thesis.

moments of institutional change are internalised and absorbed. This is not to suggest that punctuated evolution is simply a model to understand disruption. It also explains the nature of normalisation through adjustments and gradual change. In either case, the recognition is the same – that institutional change is constant and generic to the institution of news journalism, but the pattern that punctuated equilibrium takes is always the following: short-term disruption, short-term adaption, and medium- to long-term normalisation. We now need to understand what these three terms mean and how they are related to news journalism.

Before discussing each evolutionary stage in detail, two examples from the scholarly literature on news journalism shed light on this evolutionary pattern. These examples are analysed through the lens of punctuated equilibrium theory and reveal the evolutionary pattern of three stages, as described above.

Example 1. Digitizing the news: innovation in online newspapers – P.J. Boczkowski

In his 2004 book, Boczkowski examines the move of news to online environments and how newspapers adapted to the new situation. The author takes a historical approach by looking not only at the ongoing transformations in the artifact, but also the related dynamics that occurred before the said artifact came into being (2004, p. 9). As he rightly argues, 'the conditions for the cultural consequences of its use start being created long before its initial deployment' (2004, p. 9), further highlighting this book's argument that changes to an institution (punctuations) occur as responses to an ongoing crisis.

Additionally, Boczkowski (2004, p. 2) attempted to look at the contextual trends, by exploring the merging of 'existing social and material infrastructures with novel technical capabilities'. This approach, of focusing on the process rather solely on the outcomes, brought to the surface the author's evolutionary thinking on how innovations are

34 Punctuated equilibrium: disruption, adaption and normalisation

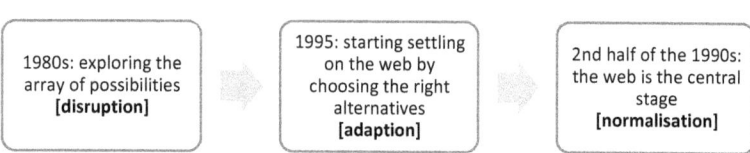

Figure 2.2 Disruption, adaption, normalisation: example 1.

'unfolding in a more gradual and ongoing fashion' and how they are shaped by 'various combinations of initial conditions [punctuations] and local contingencies' (2004, p. 4). That is to say, that apart from looking at the initial disruption (the process of emerging) and the process of adaption, there is a need to look also at the next stage when the actual use of a technology is implemented (normalisation) and when uneven (not uniform) appropriations of the technology occur (2014, p. 178).

When it comes to online newspapers, the author (2004, p. 14) explains that the 1980s was the decade of exploration, when 'dailies tinkered with a diversity of delivery vehicles, information infrastructures, and content options, and they learned about the commercial feasibility of these endeavours by studying how users responded to them'. Moving on, 'the first half of the 1990s saw a progressive narrowing of non-print alternatives, and by 1995 American dailies had settled on the web as their consumer-oriented information environment of choice' (2004, p. 14).

Using punctuated equilibrium as an analytical model (Disruption – Adaption – Normalisation) Boczkowski's analysis[6] of the integration of online technologies and online formats and innovative strategies into journalistic practices reveals the following (Figure 2.2).

Example 2. The platform press (Tow center for digital journalism, Columbia University)

The Tow Center for Digital Journalism at Columbia's Graduate School of Journalism published three reports (in three consecutive years: 2017, 2018, 2019), focusing on the influence of social media platforms and technology companies on American journalism. Through the analysis of the reports holistically and comparatively, it is possible to discern the relationship between platforms and news organisations/

Punctuated equilibrium: disruption, adaption and normalisation 35

publishers through an evolutionary prism that includes our three distinct stages: disruption, adaption and normalisation. For this reason, I linked every report with a respective stage: report 1 – disruption; report 2 – adaption; report 3 – normalisation.

Stage 1. Disruption: the topic of the first report is 'How Silicon Valley Re-engineered Journalism' (2017). In this, Bell and Owen, point to the non-neutrality of platforms and the ways these platforms impose their publishing power on news organisations. In this stage, there is a high involvement of platform companies in influencing news production. New values, such as virality, are emerging. Additionally, even though the essential nature of journalism has not changed, 'it is threaded through a system built for scale, speed and revenue' (2017, p. 15). In other words, in a system that favours scale and shareability, design standards and materiality gain a prominent role.

Stage 2. Adaption: the second report is called 'Friend and Foe: The Platform Press at the Heart of Journalism'. In this, Rashidian et al. (2018) discuss how technology platforms lean into the role of publisher and become even more enmeshed in the journalistic ecosystem, by being 'more explicitly editorial in their own practices and structures'. The reactions by news organisations are dual: on one hand, they are engaged with social media platforms by adapting their practices to social media news environments. On the other, they are 'showing signs of pushing back with strategies that help them retain some autonomy and control' (2018, pp. 3–4). In a way, they are attempting to bring audiences back to their own platforms (e.g., their websites). However, newsrooms are 'increasing oriented toward understanding and leveraging platforms as part of finding a sustainable future' and there is an evident 'rapid and ongoing merging in the functions of news publishers and platforms' (2018).

Stage 3. Normalisation: In the third report, named 'Platforms and Publishers: The End of an Era', Rashidian et al. (2019) observe a shift in the relationship between platforms and news publishers and a change at the ethos of their collaboration, even though news publishers continue to rely on a variety of platform products. To this end, they record two key tendencies: (a) news publishers are adjusting to their readers' needs – in the so-called 'post-scale era', they note that 'success necessitates regaining control of revenue streams and putting core audience interests above platform demands', and (b) platforms are adjusting to news publishers, who are now using social media platforms mainly as 'marketing vehicles' (2019) (Figure 2.3).

```
┌─────────────────────┐   ┌─────────────────────┐   ┌─────────────────────┐
│ - Platform companies│   │ - Platform companies│   │ - Platform companies│
│   attempt to influence│ │   lean into the role of│ │   adjust to the demands of│
│   news production   │   │   publisher.        │   │   news publishers   │
│ - News publishers   │   │ - News publishers   │   │ - News publishers   │
│   explore new design│   │   engage with social media│ │   prioritise their readers'│
│   standards that affect│ │   platforms; adjust their│ │   need instead of │
│   types of content  │   │   practices; but do not│  │   conforming to platforms'│
│   [disruption]      │   │   unequivocally accept│   │   affordances       │
│                     │   │   influence.        │   │   [normalisation]   │
│                     │   │   [adaption]        │   │                     │
└─────────────────────┘   └─────────────────────┘   └─────────────────────┘
```

Figure 2.3 Disruption, adaption, normalisation: example 2.

2.1.1 Punctuated equilibrium stage 1: short-term disruption

There are two dimensions to disruption: one is displacement, the other is the commonplace nature of disruption.

Disruption as a displacement event

The disruption of news journalism organisations by communication technology is premised on the straightforward idea and materialist notion that by 'retooling' journalism and by at the same time ensuring that audiences are simultaneously also 'retooled',[7] the marketplace for information will be expanded to the mutual economic and civil benefits of everyone concerned. Twitter adopted this type of thinking when it positioned itself as a journalistic platform that would respond to specific needs, primarily that of immediacy. This is perfectly captured in Evan Williams' (Twitter's co-founder) words, in August 2009:

> It is [Twitter] not necessarily journalism, certainly not in the classic case, but it does enable people to report news and events as they're happening, and often from the ground, as we just saw in Iran, people on the streets reporting what was going on, it was newsworthy content that people were tweeting, there's obviously a lot of commentary about what's going on, but it doesn't take the place of journalists or news because you still need analysis, you still need verification of this information. But it adds another layer to the information ecosystem.
>
> (Williams, 2009, as cited in Arthur 2009)

At the same time audiences were conceived as citizens or consumers entitled to a more participatory role in news journalism. This conception was already apparent, especially during the 'blog era', when emphasis was placed on the collaborative creation and existence of blurring boundaries between audiences and journalists – or the 'formerly known as media audiences' as Rosen (2007) coined them (Papacharissi, 2014, p. 34). However, as discussed in Chapter 1, audiences' role became even more prominent due to Twitter.

In other words, short-term disruption was accompanied by the promise that the role of news journalism would be enhanced and its civil power[8] would be extended. Under the rubric of this promise, short-term disruption was disaggregated to include both of the following claims: that there would be new forms of sourcing, disseminating and covering news and that the news journalists of the future would need to participate in a new form of a retooled public discussion. Returning to Romanelli and Tushman's (1994, p. 1143) argument that disruption leads to contradictive reactions, this is confirmed in the case of Twitter. On the one hand, it led to hyperbolic reactions concerning its dynamic, while on the other, there was a degree of resistance and scepticism towards its potential to cause fundamental changes (see below, in *adaption*).

Seymour (2019, p. 29) describes the techno-optimism that came along Twitter's emergence (during the 'disruption' stage):

> We would enjoy "creative autonomy", freed from the monopolies of old media and their own-way traffic of meaning. We would find new forms of political engagement instead of parties, connected by arborescent online networks. Multitudes would suddenly swarm and descend on the powerful, and then dissipate just as quickly, before they could be sanctioned. Anonymity would allow us to form new identities freed from the limits of our everyday lives, and escape surveillance. There were a host of so-called "Twitter revolutions", misleadingly credited to the ability of educated social industry users to outflank senile dictatorships, and discredit the 'elderly rubbish' they spoke.

This passage reflects the numerous accounts about platforms' revolutionary potential and disruption as displacement. For example, Parker et al. (2016, pp. 3, 7) regard platforms (including Twitter) as causing 'revolutionary changes' in almost every aspect of a business, and they argue that 'any industry in which information is an important ingredient is a candidate for the platform revolution'. Proclamations such as 'every major channel of information will be Twitterfied' (Johnson, 2009) reflect a degree of hyperbole about the potential of Twitter, that is quite common when new media technologies are introduced. Papacharissi (2010, pp. 7–8) calls this the 'mythology of the new', as the 'new' is greeted via 'discursive polarities of utopia and dystopia' that further reflect 'corresponding mythologies of our expectations of the new and our disillusionment with the old'. In this case, the 'new', namely Twitter, was initially seen largely through the lens of its beneficial impact. Mills et al. (2007), for example, whose study focused on the use of Twitter during breaking news events, equated Twitter with the 'ideal network' by juxtaposing its characteristics to those of Twitter.[9] Highfield's quote (2016, p. 71) is probably the most indicative of this tendency: 'If journalism has been previously seen as the "first draft of history", then Twitter is host to "the first draft of present"' (2016, p. 71). Stross notes that 'Twitter could be confronted as "the first draft of journalism"' (Stross, 2016). Essentially, social networking sites are said to bring forth 'a means of communication that is for the public by the public' and are heralded as 'novel, pervasive and conferring agency' (Fenton, 2016, p. 146).

Such accounts of Twitter, that position it as 'change-maker', echo greater narrative views of technology as consisting of 'sacred and utopian material' (Alexander, 2020). Alternatively, new media will lead us to the 'reinvention of journalism in a better form' (Curran et al., 2016, p. 22). With regard to Twitter the promise was that one form of the occupational role of news journalism was to be displaced by another (the active journalists). Old newsrooms would be displaced by new types of newsrooms (that entail greater interactivity and rapid responsiveness). One version of the marketplace would be displaced by another (a more expanded one), while one form of passive citizen/consumer relationship would be displaced by another (a more participatory one). Displacement was conceived of in purely evolutionary terms – natural growth facilitated by organic organisational changes – platforms, like Twitter, are 'gradually infiltrating in, and converging with, the (offline, legacy) institutions and practices through which democratic societies are organised' (van Dijck et al., 2018, p. 2).

News journalism organisations that adapted to the retooled marketplace of information had an edge over the competition. The main consequences of not responding to the processes of necessary displacements are that 'you are left behind' and lose a stake in the new opportunities created by, in this case, Twitter. The failure to retool is the failure to adapt and to risk losing out on commercial opportunities. As Dean Baquet (The New York Times, 2017), Executive Editor of *The New York Times*, expressed it: 'We believe that to remain the world's best news organization, we have to maintain a vibrant presence on social media'. In short, the commercial necessity for news organisations to adjust and adapt are used to justify the above forms of displacement.

The second aspect of short-term disruption that occurred at the same time as displacement was more existential concerns about how the introduction and impact of Twitter in news organisations was experienced.

2.2 Disruption as a commonplace event

Slow and simple changes may intersect with rapid and complex transformations (Moore, 1963, p. 3); thus, disruptive events are often ordinary, matters of everyday life and, if at all, matters of further concern, subject to routine repair activities within social situations (Vollmer, 2013, p. 5). These repair activities provide an opportunity for innovation. Thus, disruption can be experienced as productive and innovative. According to Vollmer (2013), many disruptions happen and attract little further notice beyond the situation in which people confront them. Only certain types of disruptions are treated as special and extraordinary and are regarded with a peculiar fascination, even by those who are not immediately concerned.

Disruption as a commonplace event emphasises that the new is based on the patterns of the old. As shown earlier with Boczkowski's (2004) study, that examined the integration of online technologies in newsrooms and the move of newspapers to online environments, the effect of the 'old' was crucial in understanding the conditions and the dynamics that led to the respective technological and social changes. Chadwick (2013, p. 8) discusses this continuity in terms of hybridity, a term that suggests 'something new that nevertheless has continuities with the old'. For example, in relation to the Internet this could be translated as the 'encouragement of the audience to inject familiar genres and routines into new and unfamiliar information environments' (Chadwick, 2013, p. 13). Similarly, for journalists this entailed the process of 'hybridising' new environments with 'their pre-existing routinized, professional practice' (Chadwick, 2017, p. 28).

Social media platforms can only be seen as emerging out of 'evolving understandings of what the web is and what "works" on it, which themselves are products of cultural, social and economic processes' (Stevenson, 2018, p. 85). In other words, 'social media must be seen as a particular constellation of previously existing ideas, values, media forms, and technologies' (Stevenson, 2018, p. 69). Understandably, people use existing values to comprehend new phenomena. This explains why for example, Twitter was initially compared to blogs. The similarities are evident if we look at the main characteristics of blogs: they are easy-to-use systems that consist of a series of personal entries that are displayed in 'reverse-chronological' order. Commenting is one of their standard features, as readers are invited to leave comments beneath each entry, responding to both the author and each other (Standage, 2013, p. 226). Besides, Twitter belongs to social networking sites but is also a form of microblogging,[10] which is largely considered the successor of blogging, and its integration into journalistic practices 'has largely mirrored the path of earlier new media technologies such as blogging' (Hermida, 2014, p. 362). Interestingly, in blogs and Twitter, we observe that the same news journalism values (see below) were challenged, highlighting once again the evolutionary thread that is common to both bringing about the need for news journalism to adjust its values system.

In their 2007 research on Twitter, Java et al. (2007) discussed this evident continuity with blogs, by spotting two differences: (a) shorter posts which lower users' requirement of time and thought investment for content generation, and (b) frequency of updates. What is interesting here though is their framing: they are using an established mode of communication to understand an emerging platform. And to do that, they are relying on the notion of continuation – or, evolution. Thus, it is not strange that early discussions of Twitter in mainstream media show that it is framed 'within the context of established journalism's norms and values' (Hermida, 2010, p. 299). Besides, their reaction towards Twitter, especially during Twitter's early years, is telling. Media organisations' use of the platform mirrored that of their adoption of the Internet during the 1990s, when websites replicated the newspaper edition. The majority of their tweets in their main institutional accounts consisted of headlines and links to news stories published on their websites, with the headlines being the same on their tweets and their websites (Armstrong & Gao, 2010; Dagoula 2012, 2017). In other words, they used Twitter as a promotional tool to drive traffic to their websites (Messner et al., 2011). This practice of using a new platform as a free and easy-to-use distribution channel for news content is reminiscent of the early years of the web, when the first journalistic websites were mostly copies of the newspapers' printed versions. Deuze (1999, p. 374) uses the term 'shovelware' to refer to the print content recycled for the web. With Twitter, these institutional accounts reduced their existence to a refined version of clickbait (Dagoula, 2017).

Murthy (2018, p. 22, 194) sees Twitter as a stage in a historical line of communication shifts in public short-messaging services. He also argues that Twitter resembles early social sharing technologies, as it could be regarded as 'a digital throwback to the analogue succinctness of telegrams' (2016, p. x); however, it differs by being free to use, public, multicast, multimedia, interactive and networked (2016, p. 19). Standage (2013, p. 250) makes a similar argument by suggesting that social media 'has been around for centuries'. By equating blogs to pamphlets and microblogs to new coffeehouses, he adds 'they are all shared, social platforms that enable ideas to travel from one person to another, rippling through networks of people connected by social bonds, rather than having to squeeze through the privileged bottleneck of broadcast media' (Standage, 2013, p. 250). Twitter as part of a historical continuum arguably continues an expansion in time and space 'along the spectrum that originated with early writing' (Murthy, 2018, p. 194). As Murthy adds, 'if email moved us exponentially up the spectrum, communicating via Twitter and similar social media represents another enormous expansion of the spectrum in terms of instantaneous, global and multiplexed communication' (Murthy, 2018, p. 194).

Similarly, some other elements can also be seen through the lens of evolution. The publicity entailed in Twitter communication, for example, is similarly not new since the boundary between public and private has been already shifted through the technological mediation of everyday messages (Murthy, 2018, p. 21). Likewise, when it comes to the transformation of news, this has already been happening through the development of online platforms in the late 1990s, that led to a history of 'unbundling' and 're-bundling' of news content, audiences and advertising (van Dijck et al., 2018, p. 51). Additionally, with regard to audiences' engagement, 'citizen or symbiotic modes of reporting' were apparent even before the arrival of social networks, with The Guardian and the BBC Hub devoting efforts and resources to explore these (García de Torres et al., 2011, p. 4). Finally, regarding pressures or editorial interference to journalists' work to enhance their performance or competitive strengths, these are 'well documented in the pre-Twitter and pre-internet era' and 'speak to the long-running contests over report autonomy' (Chadha & Wells, 2016, p. 1032).

This argumentation about social change in relation to technological change as an evolutionary process highlights the aspect of continuation and simultaneously the notion that disruption can be a commonplace event that occurs as part of this evolution. As Zelizer (2019, p. 345) notes, 'each new large technological advancement in journalism has been received as a matter of course as if civilization were about to begin from anew, even as it wipes away the ongoing and incremental nature of technological change (...)'. The material impact of Twitter was absorbed both symbolically and culturally into the categories of understandings of the traditional role of news journalism. There was no clash of cultures between the old and the new, rather the routinisation of the new within broadly speaking the categories that define what news journalism is. This is not to say that displacement did not entail the shock of the new, but rather the accommodation of new forms of adjustment and early-stage adaption. Clearly not every journalist felt comfortable or believed that it was necessary to use Twitter, as I discuss in the next section that unpacks pathways to adaption. Nevertheless, its use has continued to expand and the consensus concerning what news journalism involves remains more or less what it always has been.

Thus, there is a contradiction between the hopes and fears that are projected on new technologies, that are captured by the respective utopian and dystopian polarities (Papacharissi, 2010). Hopes are linked to the convergence of social media and journalism and the ways this convergence would create 'a superior or hybrid version of both' – Bell and Owen (2017, p. 14) describe this as 'a rich network populated by useful and timely information, which could be easily augmented, shared and commented on by a highly engaged population'. However, as the authors add, the situation was quite the opposite as 'the worst elements of both worlds have combined, tainting the old and the new media' (Bell & Owen, 2017, p. 14).

Importantly, in assessing the role of Twitter we need to ensure not to over- or underestimate its impact (Jungherr et al., 2020), but to contextualise it in terms of the commonplace nature of the displacement activities described above. This is also connected to the fact that the impact of disruptions covers both displacement and commonplace elements; therefore, we need to bear this in mind when assessing the costs and benefits of Twitter's disruption of news journalism.

2.1.2 Punctuated equilibrium stage 2: short-term adaption

At the level of meso-sociology, institutions are a subsystem of the social system that according to Parsons (1971) must meet systemic functional prerequisites. For Parsons, this means that an institution or subsystem must be able to cope successfully with change if it is not to suffer dysfunctional consequences, e.g., internal strains and/or insufficient adaptation to external environments. In short, institutions and the organisations that comprise them need to adapt and integrate both to macro- and meso-level changes through the processes of adaption. The key to sustaining institutional life lies in the adaptive capacity of all institutions and their constituent organisations.

In other words, within the institutional framework of news journalism, constituent news organisations have to adopt adaptive strategies that while they can vary must nevertheless conform to their own institutionally based value systems of journalistic norms and mores if they are to remain within the purview of what it is to do institutionally defined news journalism. Adaption does not therefore mean the active transformation of these institutional values but rather ensuring that conformity to these values both preserves and extends them. That is, they must retain their core meaning and at the same adjust to challenges to traditional ways of going about news journalism. In this, they provide a context for news organisation to meet the practical demands these challenges occasion.

To return to Parsonian (1971) functionalist language, adaptation is a response to disruption, but is an essentially short-term process that eventually leads to integration (when the institution and its component organisation meets the conditions to maintain its analytically defined boundaries in relation to its external environments), and to latency (when the institution and its component organisation meets the conditions to preserve actors' motivations, knowledge, norms and values). Failing to adapt (or respond to the disruption) compromises the stability of the institution and its component organisation or even its survival. News organisations attempt to develop, adopt and utilise new technologies to survive in a competitive market and to remain relevant (Min & Fink, 2021; *New York Times Innovation Report*, 2014 as cited in Benton, 2014). The introduction of Twitter into news organisations constituted the process of readjusting practices, structures and processes to best make use of the affordances[11] provided by Twitter (Jungherr et al., 2020).

There is a plethora of factors at play when it comes to the adaptation of social media platforms by news organisations. Integration into journalistic practices 'is not determined by the technological innovation solely, but it is a social process of appropriation' (Gulyas, 2013, p. 283). What this suggests is that the extent and scope of journalists' adaptive processes to disruption in their news organisation varies according to their role, age, understanding of their job, seniority and education. Also significant is the size and complexity of the organisation they are working for, its culture and history as well as economic factors concerning ownership and corporate mission. Adapting to Twitter and integrating it into their professional routines created new professional divides among journalists (Hedman & Djerf-Pierre, 2013, p. 381). A summary of the main categorisations of adaptive processes adopted by news journalists and thought to be significant in the way Twitter was adapted to, is presented in Table 2.1.

The table shows the different understandings of the process of adaption, while they also undoubtedly overlap in places. Each one can be

44 Punctuated equilibrium: disruption, adaption and normalisation

Table 2.1 Categorisation of journalists based on their uses and perceptions of Twitter (from the most resistant to less)

Hedman & Djerf-Pierre (2013)	Revers (2014)	Rogstad (2014)	Hedman (2016)	Gulyas (2016)	Mellado & Alfaro (2020)
The sceptical shunners	Traditionalists	The sceptics	The sceptical tweeters	Sceptics	Sceptical Resistant
The pragmatic conformists	Light tweeters Sceptics	The networkers	The enthusiastic tweeters	Observers	The adapted approach
The enthusiastic activists	Intense tweeters Enthusiasts	The two-faced		Hunters	The redefiner approach
		The opiners		Promoters	
		The sparks		Architects	

examined in terms of what they reveal about adaptive competencies and strategies. In essence, how journalists coped.

Hedman and Djerf-Pierre (2013, p. 381) identified three coping strategies. The first is the sceptical shunners, who generally avoid social media and are deeply sceptical of its impact on the way news journalism is undertaken and therefore of its relevance to them. Typically, this category is represented by older journalist working in newspapers. The second coping strategy is that deployed by the pragmatic conformists. They are regular users of social media who are selective and judicious in their usage of all social media. They are ambivalent about using social media, as they see it as both a valuable journalistic tool and at the same time they are not entirely convinced about the virtues of audience adaptation, personal branding and of using the platforms in a personal capacity. This ambivalence manifests itself by their willingness to use social media simply for information scanning and news gathering, but not for frequent posting. They do use the platforms though due to imposed expectations 'by perceived peer pressure and organizational requirements' – in other words, they feel that they are 'expected to be up to date with the current trends in the industry and believe that cultivating their social media skills is a professional requirement' (2013, p. 381). In this category, we find journalists from all age groups and workplaces. The third coping strategy is that of the enthusiastic activists. They are journalists that have fully embraced social media. Apart from scanning for information, they frequently use social media for networking, personal branding and collaboration. They perceive and value social media as highly disruptive and a positive force for generating significant changes to the profession of journalism.

Similarly, Gulyas' (2016, p. 404) research, which uses interviews with journalists and surveys, also categorises journalists by their coping strategy. For Gulyas (2016), there are five groups (architects, promoters, hunters, observers and sceptics) that again highlight that 'social media adoption is not homogenous, and the tools are appropriated into specific contexts of individual journalists utilizing social media affordances' and that they span a range from doubt to acceptance to enthusiasm.

In similar fashion to the above two studies, Rogstad (2014, pp. 694–695) identifies five clusters of journalists based on their social media coping strategies, namely the sceptics, the networkers, the two-faced, the opiners and the sparks. Her research concerns political news journalists, and specifically the members of the Norwegian Parliamentary Press Gallery. Sceptics believe that the emphasis on metrics of popularity, self-promotion and personal branding and audience engagement are unimportant. 'Networkers' prioritise and value being part of an intra-elite network facilitated by Twitter but not its populist or personal aspects. Whereas 'opiners' value Twitter because it allows them to express their opinions constantly. The 'two-faced' are similar to the pragmatic conformists described above. And as for the sparks, they resemble the 'enthusiastic activists' described above, in that they lead an online life and they use social media extensively and consider likes and comments as important indicators for how their work and persona is perceived.

Revers (2014) refers to journalists who use Twitter as coping in three ways. First, intense tweeters or enthusiasts to capture those who embraced a whole range of tweeting practices. This group considered a tweet 'as a segment within a flow of news discourse, which they assessed holistically' and regarded professional norms as having to change to meet the demands of Twitter and journalists' new roles. Second, the 'light tweeters or sceptics' who advertised their own stories on Twitter, but were more restrained when it came to promoting others' news stories, live tweeting, commenting and conversing. Third, the 'traditionalists' who were outspoken critics of Twitter and 'exercised an institutional resilience, which aimed at reproducing the logic of professional control and aspired to keep journalism as autonomous as possible' (2014, p. 812). They regarded the news as a 'closed entity' that accords to specific standards; hence, tweets are not news. Regarding professional norms traditionalists conceive of journalism as having extant established norms applicable to Twitter. To deviate from these norms is for them equivalent to undermining professional news journalism.

Likewise, Mellado and Alfaro (2020, p. 1266) focus on how journalists in Chile perceive their professional identity in relation to their Twitter and Instagram use. Unlike the other studies, they focus on how journalists understand their own digital selves. They identify three such digital selves. First, the adapted who define their digital identity and roles through traditional roles and values, the sceptical or resistant who believe that their professional digital identity does not need to adjust or accommodate the mentality that is imposed by social media and, finally, the 'redefiners' who express digital identities, and the roles of their profession, through their social media activity and use (Mellado & Alfaro, 2020, p. 1266) via their personal engagement with Twitter and their interaction with their audiences.

In essence, all the above studies point to how coping strategies (and by extension digital selves) and adapting to the impact of Twitter are

Punctuated equilibrium: disruption, adaption and normalisation 47

broadly similar: they follow patterns of 'accept-adjust-reject'. However, whatever coping strategy is adopted as a form of short-term adaption it remains the case that journalists are constrained by organisational pressures and contingencies, by changing institutional norms and values, and by the extent to which they have independence from these considerations. Equally all the above coping strategies are varieties of short-term adaption utilised to ameliorate or ignore Twitter. Over time, coping strategies become attenuated and normalisation occurs.

2.1.3 Punctuated equilibrium stage 3: medium- and long-term normalisation

Normalisation in news organisations and within the institution of news journalism is best understood as the process of adhering to current norms and practices and by maintaining the institution's analytically established boundaries, as well as adjusting to some elements of change through specialisation, role differentiation and the adoption of new particularised functions (Moore, 1963, p. 108). In other words, the continuation of those adaptive practices deemed by news organisation to be both retaining core values while extending them to include those elements of change seen to be appropriate to undertaking news journalism. In other words, adjusting the shared understandings of the roles, norms and values of news journalism, while adapting the process of disruption. In brief, normalisation occurs through various levels of adjustments, and 'imperceptibly through gradual transformations of the user habits and changing levels of acceptance' (van Dijck, 2013, p. 19). Overall, for the institution of news journalism to be considered as integrated or normalised means that, value systems that govern behaviours are consistent and coordinated, and that the institution retains its integrity and influence on news organisations.

Examples of this process of normalisation abound in the study of professional norms in news journalism and news media. Resnick, for example, captures the process of normalisation by referring to the 'normalisation of the Internet' in relation to political activity, suggesting that 'as more and more political actors move online, the Internet becomes dominated by the usual offline interests' (Resnick, cited in Siapera, 2012, p. 86). Singer (2005) focuses on how blogs have become normalised by looking at how political journalists attempted to fit blogging into their traditional professional norms and practices. Singer notes that 'the blog is being normalised as a component and, in some ways, an enhancement of traditional journalistic norms and practices', as journalists 'continue to think in terms of their professional role as information providers as they migrate to the interactive online medium'. Lasorsa et al. (2012), drawing on Singer's work, performed an extensive content analysis of journalists' tweets (j-tweeters) to examine whether the process of normalisation was applicable to Twitter and concluded that in this arena, the process was two-way: j-tweeters vary widely in their use of the platform, but they appear to be normalising microblogs to fit into their norms and practices. What is more, they simultaneously appear to be adjusting these norms and practices to Twitter's evolving ones (2012, p. 31). These and similar studies illustrate the ways professional norms of detachment, impartiality, gatekeeping and curating the news, as well as the processes of verification and traditional mores of who a news journalist is accountable to, are challenged and accommodated. And the ways in which news journalism has had to relinquish its gatekeeping role into one of gatewatching by adjusting to the conventions and practices that are prescribed in the Twittersphere. This latter point is important simply because it prefigures what ultimately counts as news. Therefore, it is used as an example here.

Hermida (2013, p. 302) notes that 'journalists and editors seek to retain a gatekeeping role, despite some opening up to the audience', by deciding what news to disseminate to audiences (Russell, 2019, p. 93). In a similar vein, Molyneux (2015, p. 921) sees the use of retweets as a means for journalists to act as gatekeepers as they have the chance to exercise their judgement through the curation of their Twitter streams. Viewing gatekeeping through the lens of news sourcing and through the embedding of tweets in news reporting, McGregor and Molyneux (2020, p. 599) point out that in this case gatekeeping consists of the decisions journalists make regarding what content and whose voices 'pass through the mythic gates'. This suggests a shift from traditional modes of gatekeeping to news judgement, essentially the filter that is applied in making these decisions. This makes news judgement one of the most important norms and professional skills that journalists need to acquire.

On Twitter however, which is an open network that allows the free flow of information, the role of journalists is shifting from gatekeepers to verifiers and analysers of information that has already passed through the gates (Canter, 2014, p. 16). As mentioned earlier, Bruns (2005, 2021, p. 252) coined the term 'gatewatching' to capture how this norm has changed since the emergence of blogs. Bruns (2021, p. 252) explains gatewatching as 'the monitoring of the output gates of conventional news organisations – their websites, broadcasts, print editions and other publication channels – for news reporting, as well as the

Punctuated equilibrium: disruption, adaption and normalisation 49

referencing, citation, evaluation, critique and other use of such source materials in another outlet's own publication output'. Bruns (2021, p. 253) refers to two waves of gatewatching. The first one occurred with the emergence of blogs, whereas the second one with social networking sites, such as Twitter. The difference between the two waves is that during the first, gatewatching consisted of the solitary activities of news bloggers whereas with social networking sites it became a shared activity that enabled collective news curation to a much greater extent than ever before (Bruns, 2021, p. 254). Gatewatching alongside news curation become even more important considering platforms (and not journalists) are often taking a leading role in how news is curated, for example by affecting the type of content that becomes predominantly visible (van Dijck et al., 2018, p. 65).

However, and interestingly, Twitter also reinforces traditional practices and mores. The reliance by news journalism on intra-elite sourcing of news is, if anything, re-enforced by Twitter. For example, Artwick (2013) finds that on Twitter there is the dominance of official sources in reporting, as journalists continue to gravitate towards elite sources. Von Nordheim et al.'s work (2018, p. 821), that looks into the use of elite and non-elite sources in *The New York Times*, *The Guardian* and *Süddeutsche Zeitung* for a ten-year period, confirms this 'reinforcement hypothesis'. The authors find an increasing reliance on Twitter as a news source, although this reliance is due to an increase in elite sources (2018, p. 821). It is evident that Twitter is used by journalists as a medium to gain access to elites, either to report on or even to embed their tweets. As McGregor and Molyneux (2020, p. 600) write, 'journalists have always heavily featured elite perspectives in news stories, but Twitter offers a new, simpler means by which to access them'.

Increasingly it seems as if Twitter has become an accepted journalistic tool which can be accommodated and adjusted in terms of a system of values that enables the institution of news journalism to move forward. According to Canter (2014, p. 16), Twitter has become normalised in the psyche of the majority of journalists as a mainstream publishing platform'. Jukes (2019, p. 255) expresses the matter rather differently and notes there now exists within news journalism a more relaxed attitude towards social media, as they felt that the 'corporate panic' of early days has faded in the meantime.

Having adopted punctuated equilibrium as providing us with the historical, analytical basis and methodological premises for how to understand Twitter's impact on the institution of news journalism empirically, it is appropriate to turn to the longitudinal study that looks at the empirical evidence for the arguments made across the last two chapters. To this end, I begin with a qualitative study which involved research interviews with news journalists which explore their views about their use of Twitter and its impact on the institution of news journalism.

Notes

1 Moore (1963, p. 3, 6) notes that complexities in social change are likely to manifest themselves as tensions and strains. This is evidenced during the process of disruption. In addition, change presumes an 'underlying basis of persistence and regularity', which is manifested in the stages of adaption and normalisation.
2 Moore (1963, p. 20) classifies different types of social change, e.g., cumulative change; 'trivial' change (that does not alter the institution it concerns); threatening change (that may be resisted or suppressed); and change that is manifested through forms of selective adaptation with significant and enduring consequences. To this end, revolutionary change is explained in terms of 'then and now'. Evolutionary change that entails processes of adaptation relies on the observed differences is explained as being between 'backwardness' and 'advancement' (Moore, 1963, p. 22, 114).
3 Importantly, Moore (1963, p. 22) notes that any social system consists of three aspects: (a) actors; (b) forms; and (c) functions (that concern intended or unintended consequences).
4 Moore (1963, p. 4) argues that the observation of change takes time, as it requires knowledge of sequences of cause and effect in a temporal order. This reasoning contributed to the decision of conducting a longitudinal study in both Chapters 3 and 4.
5 Alexander et al. write that human history, despite its complexity and its contradictions, 'can be seen to fit a pattern' (2008, p. 584). This pattern is evident in Toffler's thesis, who suggests three waves of transformation: (a) the agricultural age – in this, people clustered into villages and their wealth was the land; (b) the industrial or machine age (lasted from the 18th century until the World War II) – in this wealth was land, labor and capital; (c) the information or knowledge age (current era) – in this wealth is the possession of knowledge and information (Alexander et al., 2008, p. 587; Toffler, 1970).
6 Boczkowski (2004, p. 11) examines three case studies/newsrooms that aim to exploit the web's capabilities as an information environment. The choice of the case studies does not rely on their representativeness but because 'they expressed with great intensity the dynamics involved in appropriating novel technical capabilities from the starting point of established socio-material infrastructures'. These are: The New York Times on the Web's Technology section, the Houston Chronicle's Virtual Voyager, and New Jersey Online Community Connection.
7 Jungherr et al. (2020) use the term 'retooling' with reference to politics and the ways digital media have provided political actors with 'new tools' to pursue their political needs. These tools are seen to have change the way some of politics is done.
8 For journalism's civil power, see Harrison (2019).

Punctuated equilibrium: disruption, adaption and normalisation 51

9   Mills et al. (2007) evaluate Twitter in terms of its cost, usability, mobility, reliability, speed, searchability, conversational aspects, visualization tools, modularity, popularity (and subsequent diffusion), openness, multimodality and verification tools.
10 Murthy (2013, p. 10) defines microblogging as an Internet-based service in which: (a) Users have a public profile where they broadcast short public messages and updates whether they are directed to specific user(s) or not; (b) messages become publicly aggregated together across users; and (c) users can decide whose messages they wish to receive, but not necessarily who can receive their messages" – a distinctive characteristic of Twitter as most social networking sites rely on bidirectional following.
11 Technological affordances refer to how human action is anticipated and facilitated by the design of tools, structures and technologies (Sujon, 2021).

3 What news journalists say about their uses of Twitter

3.1 Qualitative approach: research interviews

This chapter outlines the qualitative part of the study, namely a set of semi-structured interview questions posed to news journalists to assess what they consider to be the impact of Twitter upon their practices, norms, mores and professional routines. These semi-structured questions formed the basis of 22 interviews in the United Kingdom and Greece conducted over the period of 2017–2022 and featured the following types of journalists (Table 3.1).

Table 3.1 List of journalists interviewed

Occupation	Nature of organisation	Gender	Code	Code translation
Journalist	Legacy	M	R1	Respondent 1
Journalist	Legacy	M	R2	Respondent 2
Journalist	Legacy	M	R3	Respondent 3
Journalist	Legacy	M	R4	Respondent 4
Journalist	Legacy	M	R5	Respondent 5
Journalist	Legacy	M	R6	Respondent 6
Journalist	Legacy	M	R7	Respondent 7
Journalist	Legacy	F	R8	Respondent 8
Journalist	Legacy	F	R9	Respondent 9
Journalist	Legacy	F	R10	Respondent 10
Journalist	Legacy	F	R11	Respondent 11
Journalist	Legacy	F	R12	Respondent 12
Journalist	Legacy	F	R13	Respondent 13
Journalist	Legacy	F	R14	Respondent 14
Journalist	Legacy & Net-native	F	R15	Respondent 15
Journalist	Legacy & Net-native	M	R16	Respondent 16
Journalist	Net-native	M	R17	Respondent 17
Journalist	Net-native	M	R18	Respondent 18
Journalist	Net-native	M	R19	Respondent 19
Journalist	Net-native	M	R20	Respondent 20
Journalist	Net-native	F	R21	Respondent 21
Journalist	Net-native	M	R22	Respondent 22

DOI: 10.4324/9781003231776-4

What news journalists say about their uses of Twitter 53

The questions posed in the interviews were organised around the three stages of punctuated equilibrium (disruption, short-term adaption, and medium- to long-term normalisation) discussed in Chapter 2. These three stages were thematised to provide the basis for the questions asked. These themes cover a variety of specific subjects that were deemed to be key indicators of change and routine in institutional news journalism. They also form the basis of how this group of news journalists experienced at firsthand the processes of disruption, adaption and normalisation. Combined they therefore give us an 'insider's account' of whether Twitter has caused a significant change to news journalism, and particularly to journalists' practices, norms, mores and professional routines. It is from this account that we can uncover how this group of news journalists saw and evaluated the institutional outcomes for news journalism, and subsequently how they saw the direct and indirect costs and benefits to news journalism.

3.2 Questionnaire themes concerning the evolutionary impact of Twitter on news journalism

3.2.1 Disruption – Theme 1a: has Twitter fundamentally changed news journalism?

This theme explores how disruptive Twitter was when it emerged and introduced to the journalists' workplaces and newsrooms and how if at all it entailed the displacement of traditional practices with new ones. The ways Twitter affected news cycles, news sourcing, news gathering and the nature of the interviewed journalists' engagement with their audience were particular foci of concern. In brief, this theme looks at how rapidly simple changes and complex transformations became commonplace.

Interestingly, all interviewees reacted similarly to the question of whether Twitter has fundamentally changed news journalism. In the first instance, they all quickly responded that Twitter has changed news journalism because of its immediacy and instantaneity. They emphasised how Twitter facilitated a quicker news cycle, faster news gathering, and extremely quick news dissemination. R4 commented on this that:

> in a pre-digital world, we were operating on a 24-hour news cycle and the papers published a story which did or did not get followed up on by the broadcasters. And now, it feels to me, working in a social media environment, that you can go through, kind of, three

news cycles before lunchtime and a story will come up and get knocked down and come up and get knocked down again, and that's just the Internet in a way, not exclusively Twitter, but Twitter is where most of that is happening for journalists, so yeah, it's been huge.

Following on and related to this initial emphasis on immediacy and instantaneity issues of how faster news gathering and quick news dissemination entailed negative and deep changes to traditional news practices were raised.

On the negative side, journalists referred to a diffused toxicity that could be disorientating (R1); to Twitter's dramatic effect on setting and controlling the news agenda (R8); to its effect on turning journalistic work into being more passive (R17); to its effect on encouraging disinformation and manipulation of public opinion within the platform (R17); and to the overwhelming number of fragments of information that makes news gathering on the platform quite demanding (R5). R2 also highlighted the aspect of constant branding of the self as he sees Twitter to be:

> turning into a bit of a glorified LinkedIn from a journalistic perspective in that it is just you showcasing the work you are doing which is then seen by other journalists, and I am not sure how much that is actually cut-through and seen by the public.

On the positive side, Twitter was seen as fundamentally changing news journalism because it constitutes a 'valuable newswire' in terms of news gathering; because it allows news journalists to find information that may be unavailable otherwise (R7); because it provides journalists with the opportunity to be constantly connected with other news journalists (R3); and because it offers a way to gain proximity to elites and political actors (R15). For R4, Twitter is considered 'the most important invention since the telephone' adding that:

> there are other forms of social media and Web 2.0 interactivity, but Twitter is the one most favoured by journalists and it has opened up the public space to people who basically did not have access to it before, in terms of central voices and sources.

All of the journalists interviewed considered Twitter to have brought changes to the profession and to have disrupted traditional journalistic practices and values, though the majority of them resisted the idea

What news journalists say about their uses of Twitter 55

of substantial changes, in spite of comments that described fundamental change. One reason for this seemingly contradictory position is because the majority of journalists interviewed distinguished between Twitter as a professional tool that affected various processes such as news gathering and its other uses: for instance, when it came to audiences it was of minority interest (and use). Where audiences were concerned, they though that the vast majority of the population did not use Twitter. In other words, Twitter served and was representative of a sub-population that consisted of fellow journalists, politicians, and well-informed citizens (R15). And while Twitter had disrupted (at first) some traditional forms of news sourcing, news gathering and news dissemination, this did not bring with it any substantially enhanced level of interaction with audiences. Similarly, other journalists (R2, R11, R13, R16) expressed their hesitance to engage with other Twitter users, unless they felt the need to respond to pressing questions.

3.2.2 Short-term adaption – Theme 2a: Can journalists now do their job without Twitter?

This theme is concerned with the journalists' attitudes to Twitter and whether there are general attitudes that reveal a more or less sceptical, pragmatic or enthusiastic approach toward using the platform. Journalists also reflected on whether they cannot do their job without Twitter. In other words, interviewees considered whether they have adjusted to Twitter and how integral they think Twitter has become for news journalism.

The majority of journalists initially pointed out the positive changes that Twitter had brought to the journalistic profession; however, they all agreed that they could do their everyday job without Twitter. That Twitter may have enhanced certain processes (sourcing and scoping investigations), but it did not alter the traditional skill sets of what constituted a well-sourced or professionally undertaken piece of journalism. Essentially, journalism was an art form and Twitter a tool. Even so, they all noted that not having Twitter as part of their toolkit would pose significant limitations, especially in terms of missing out pieces of crucial information or being slower in their coverage and reporting. For example, R10 considered Twitter as an integral tool for any journalist that wants to be well-informed about the current agenda and 'trends', and about last-minute information that is circulated firstly on Twitter. Likewise, R22 thought that all media organisations should have a 'special unit' as part of a broader team that would work to investigate and verify information on social media platforms.

Similarly, R5's words capture this overall feeling:

> I think it's still possible. It's still possible because you can still ask for things to be sent over email. You can still talk to people on phones. You can still go out and do things in person. But if you remove that key tool from your job, then it's going to make it ten times harder for you to access information and this is because a lot of stuff that we report on now or get material for comes from social media. It's just a fact.
>
> (R5)

For R5, being able to research information online, network and to connect with diverse sources Twitter was essential:

> I think they (journalists) could still do the job, but it would be considerably harder because social media is where a lot of people are now. And a lot of people are sharing their stories and sharing their lives and sharing photos of their lives. If you remove that key tool from your job, then it's going to it's going to make it ten times harder for you to access information. Because a lot of stuff that we report on now, or get material from, comes from social media. It's just a fact.

In a similar vein, R22 highlighted that 'Twitter is, until now at least, the best journalistic tool to monitor information'.

Others pointed out that there are other tools that are equally useful. For instance, R2, R12 and R13 considered Facebook as the most important social networking platform for them. This choice is also connected with the particulars of their job, as was the case for journalists that work on a local or regional level, Facebook is seen as the primary way to gain access to local and regional communities. As R2 noted:

> I don't think from the local, regional level that I work at, you can get away with not using Facebook, because there are just so many gems there. There's local groups for everything and the more niche you go, the more interesting people you speak to. I've gotten some incredible stories just from spotting something on Facebook and, as a result of that, have been the first to break it and got an exclusive.

Facebook was also regarded by many journalists as the best tool to organise their networks with other journalists (R2, R10, R11, R12,

R13). Apart from Facebook, others referred to other, more traditional tools (such as the phone).

Interestingly, some connected the choice of the right platform with the type of reporting they are working on. For instance, for R21, who covers political issues, pointed out that not using Twitter would be a limitation as this could lead to missing out on important information, especially because nowadays political actors use Twitter as their only direct communication channel.

Overall, though, the majority of interviewees saw Twitter only as another piece of the puzzle that constitutes their journalistic routine, 'a part of the job, but not the whole job' (R1). To this end, most of them referred to Twitter as an additional 'tool', and emphasised that regardless of the tools or the platforms one uses, the most integral parts of the journalistic work is to have a solid network and to know how to investigate a topic (for example: R11, R12, R15, R19). Twitter as a tool is only necessary for the job – highly useful and time saving, possibly enhancing on some occasions the accuracy and depth of information needed a story but not substantially altering the skill set necessary for being a news journalist.

3.2.3 Short-term adaption – Theme 2b: The role of formal and informal training in the use of Twitter

Adaption here is looked at in terms of formal and informal coping strategies through acquiring an understanding of how to use Twitter should they need to or be required to, and how these coping strategies are deployed by journalists in situ. Questions focused on how did they come to understand Twitter and how did they adapt and adjust their own practices to Twitter.

Interestingly, none of the interviewees had received formal training related to the use of social media, or Twitter specifically. For some journalists training occurred through their unofficial discussions with other journalists, or along the way, by 'picking up things while using the platforms' (R2). For R3, the process was a natural progress from blogs, noting that 'at the beginning, I thought I was talking to myself, but actually, you know, there were some people who were interested in that'. After the newspaper he is working for linked blogs to Twitter, he decided to 'give it a go'.

> It was just by chance that I bumped into a member of the parliament and he said "I like your tweets" and I didn't know what he was talking about, because it was an automatic feed from the blog to Twitter and it would just tweet the headline of the blog with the

link to it. I looked at Twitter and I saw that I had 600 followers and I thought "Oh this is quite interesting". So, I started tweeting and I have been doing it absolutely constantly twenty-four hours a day ever since. That's what it feels like anyway.

Interestingly all journalists (apart from R16) thought that it was absolutely necessary to have some formal 'quality' training that enables a deeper use of Twitter and that enables them from just seeing Twitter in terms of a tool for attracting wider audiences. The things they thought were most important areas for training included: how to use Twitter for live coverage of events; how to best exploit Twitter's features, such as the feature of lists; how to interact with audiences; how to best monitor and filter information; how to manage an information tide during a crisis; how to increase their tweet's visibility; and how to integrate Twitter in their journalistic practices in a non-time-consuming way.

For a journalist working for a traditional newspaper that has a very strong digital presence, formal training so far equates to concrete social media guidelines. Even though it is not really training, but 'sensible guidelines like "don't lie to anyone on Twitter, don't engage with the trolls, don't give out your personal address"' (R4). Similarly, R4 added that social media guidelines suggest that 'journalists represent the newspaper on Twitter and therefore anything they tweet will be taken as representative of the newspaper' and he observed that 'that's a role that people adopt relatively effectively'. For R4, this is a matter that is directly linked to the aims of the news organisation. As he noted 'there was a stage, five to ten years ago, when you went to a job interview, people would look at how many Twitter followers you got, the more the better', however, there was a shift:

> I think within news organizations, they started to row back and think, "Actually, do we really want our journalists spending all their time doing this?" (...). You build up profiles like that by having many people tweeting inflammatory sorts of content to attract attention. I am fairly sure that the editors started thinking "Well actually, is that really what we want? We want a big platform for our journalism and if we're tweeting a link to a story, we'd rather have someone with a million followers to tweet that than someone with a hundred followers, but do we really want all of our journalists spending time having rows with people that degenerate into unsavoury at best? Is it good for our newspaper's brand if journalists are doing this?".

For R16 though, having guidelines for training feels somewhat restrictive, similar to getting instructions on what to say or what to wear in your work environment. Even so, all journalists agreed that the best way to get acquainted with Twitter is by using it and by learning through mistakes and errors.

3.2.4 Short-term adaption – Theme 2c: The changing nature of the journalist's relationship with audiences

This theme is concerned with how journalists adopted for themselves a professional and personal digital self. Professionally, this meant how they presented themselves to their audiences on Twitter, how they adjusted to their new relationships with their audiences, and how this adjustment affected their work. Personally, this meant how they use Twitter in their personal capacity. However, it does need to be noted that on Twitter the boundaries between the personal and the professional are blurred and crossovers from one to the other mode of presenting oneself are constant and often not clear-cut.

3.2.4.1 Professional engagement

All journalists considered Twitter as a platform that changed their relationship with their audiences. Interestingly, when reflecting on this relationship, the majority of journalists diverged to discuss how Twitter can be a toxic environment that encourages abuse, attacks and targeting, as considered later. Overall, though, responding to audiences or engaging with them was seen as an additional pressure that adds to the demands of their everyday job. R5 explained that Twitter is 'also about having a kind of presence as well and being able to promote your work' adding that 'because you're a journalist as a public facing job and part of the public facing part of it now is online, is on social media'. While R7 mentioned that he sometimes feels overwhelmed by the requirements of this communication:

> I have to try to pull myself back a little bit, in terms of my engagement since I have started using Twitter. Partly that is because just naturally your number of followers grows, your audience grows and then, physically, the needed time to respond to people becomes limited. And I mean literally physically, you sit there and suddenly, you have been on Twitter for an hour and a half without realizing it. So, you have to be a little bit careful about that.
>
> (R7)

Similarly, R4 highlighted that even though he would like to be able to engage with everyone who has a sensible question, this is not realistic, due to the high number of messages he receives on a daily basis:

> I will get, probably, between two dozen to fifty or something messages or mentions on Twitter of which about a dozen or so I might engage with, probably because they're questions that demand a response. When it's just people saying "I liked that, I didn't like that" and I don't feel obliged to reply.

The number of messages he receives is significantly higher during busy days when political developments occur, and he recognises that it is impossible to engage with all messages despite wanting to do so noting that 'in a sense, that does create a sort of pressure, you feel that people out there want a reply from you but you're giving them a reply and that's disappointing'.

As mentioned earlier, journalists avoid engaging with audiences because of the possibility of getting exposed to attacks or being targeted. R2 mentioned the negative aspects of proximity to an audience – that it could on occasions expose a journalist to abuse, being targeted or even attacked – he noted:

> I'm working for reach, so anything that I do, that I publish story-wise, I need to be mindful that whatever I comment on or respond to doesn't get me into any other holes or someone could pick up on something that I say and twist it and then I'm sort of backtracked and then your reputation is very quickly tarnished.

R4 has a similar approach. In his own words: 'I don't engage with people I think aren't worth engaging with because they just want to criticise you in an insulting manner, so I kind of ignore those and don't engage with them at all'. Though this was further qualified when he added 'I mean, it's a, sort of, platform for abuse, but it's not just a platform for abuse and in terms of... I might get quality useful feedback on my journalism every day through Twitter', adding that:

> I mean if someone thinks you spelled a name wrong or that you used a word insensitively, or you've kind of missed the point or you misunderstood a statistic, they can tweet you and I tend to see those more quickly than I see my emails. And if they've got a point, as long as they are polite and sensible, I'll respond to anyone on Twitter. In that sense, it's been really good for our relationship

with readers. A lot of journalists still feel that feedback from readers and viewers is more trouble than it's worth and that it's a nuisance, but I don't, I genuinely find that being challenged in that way sharpens up my journalism every day.

R5, R19 and R21 valued Twitter for the opportunity it offers to directly reply to comments and questions. R5 and R15:

> there are people that might have a certain view because they don't have the full picture. In this case, I do try to engage, and to explain. I have tried this and it sometimes has positive effects. But to be honest, I feel that very few journalists are willing to engage in this kind of conversation, particularly because they are afraid that this will derail into some kind of toxic dialogue.

In similar vein, R21 said:

> I am one of those journalists that really like the immediacy, the instant connection. When I was working at a traditional newspaper in the past, I responded to every single email I received from our readers. And if I received letters, I would do the same. I regard Twitter the same way. I respond to everyone who has a fair comment or question, or those who address me in good faith, even if they are critical about my work. But I don't respond to malicious comments or to trolls. I simply do not engage.

On balance the possibility for meaningful engagement with audiences was still seen as desirable. But it was also seen as increasingly risky. The value of a digital self was increasingly being judged against about a background of an increasingly less civil public sphere. Correspondingly journalists judged that their professional digital selves were increasingly becoming more cautious and more concerned about negative audience.

3.2.4.2 *Personal touch*

For all journalists apart from R5, Twitter was seen as strictly a professional tool. For this reason, they emphasised that they only use Twitter within the requirements of their job. But R4 recognised that 'Twitter is operating in a grey area where, you know, journalists who work for news organisations, to what extent they're tweeting personally and to what extent they're tweeting as journalists is a matter that's unresolved'. R3 mentioned that 'it's entirely professional. It has to do with my work as a journalist. I never tweet anything personal. But I've always been like that with my journalism'. In similar fashion, R4 pointed out that 'I've never been comfortable with that because I'm relatively private and I don't want to be a public figure in that regard'. This feeling was shared by many journalists (for example, R11, R12, R13, R14, R16 and R21) who mentioned that Twitter is about the news, not about them.

Similarly, R12 noted that she would never talk about her personal life, because she considers her personal life to be irrelevant to the audiences. To this end, R12 highlighted that what should be at the centre of attention is the story and not the journalists themselves; otherwise, this might reveal 'an extreme point of unconstraint narcissism'.

Even so, R4 noted that this is a personal choice:

> I have thousands of followers on Twitter, which is okay for a journalist, but it's not a mega-platform. If I tweeted much more often about opinionated things, or used it for jokes or to discuss family things, I could probably build that audience up a lot more, but I don't want to. I don't particularly disapprove of other people doing that and I can see that people are interested in some people tweeting where they go for a walk or a nice sunset, or sort of what their puppy looks like or that they have found a nice recipe for chicken curry. I don't read all of that stuff, particularly if it's people I know, but I don't think that's anything intrinsically wrong and if you're comfortable doing these things, then it's probably good for your career, but yeah, I'm not.

Likewise, R15 regarded a personal touch as a matter of balance, as it could have both positive and negative consequences, especially on one's mental health. He added that journalism is a very difficult and demanding job and personal overexposure can easily add to those demands. He recognised though that exposing parts of their personalities might have a positive effect on journalists – for instance, it might be therapeutic for journalists, or it might allow audiences to trust them more 'by seeing journalists' personality beyond their professional competence'.

For this reason, R5 considered the personal touch to be an essential part of using Twitter:

> it's good to be personable because you can't just be a robot and just be sharing like bland things all the time. You have to kind of give it a bit of a personal edge because it allows people to relate

What news journalists say about their uses of Twitter 63

to it more, and to relate more to you as a human, otherwise, it's going to limit how much engagement you get in the work you are sharing with them.

R11 added that it is pointless to have two accounts on Twitter, a professional and a personal one, so she avoids sharing personal information. However, she was unsure whether this was the right choice. In agreement, R13 said that she was 'confused about the right approach' as even though she does not share any personal views or information, she feels that this affects her professional engagement negatively within Twitter. Reflecting on her use of the platform she thought that the personal touch would benefit her self-branding on Twitter. Self-branding and promotion were mentioned by various journalists (R17, R18, R21) as a potential positive outcome of adding their personal touch in their Twitter feeds; however, they were all hesitant in doing so, as they feel that this contradicts their role as journalists and their traditional value of centralising the story and not themselves.

3.2.5 *Normalisation – Theme 3a: Daily patterns of use*

This theme looks at how adaptive and adjusted norms and practices have become embedded and routinised in the role of news journalist and in the workings of the news organisations. In short, this theme examines what elements of change represented 'the new normal'. In ethnomethodological terms, what practices have become 'taken for granted.'

All the news journalists interviewed said that they use social media 'simply all the time,' with journalists working at a regional or local news organisation using Facebook more than they use Twitter. This was because they felt that Facebook allowed them to get greater depth on local events, more personalisation with regard to local stories and enhanced their ability to promote more effectively what they deemed to be the relevance of their stories to local interests and needs. For them, Twitter is a tool that provides them with a glimpse of global trends, the 'bigger' national picture and insights into the 'pulse' of the wider (national not local) audience (R10). Both national and regional journalists did agree that when it comes to the question of whether they feel the need to be constantly connected on Twitter they said that they did. For instance, R2 responded:

> I would say it's continual throughout the day. There isn't a working day that I don't use it. There probably isn't an hour where I don't use it. It is just there as a tool to be used in our line of work.

As for whether Twitter is part of his routine outside of his working hours, R2 replied that:

> I check it even when I finish work. Obviously it's still all there on your phone isn't it? You're still logged into all of those accounts. I still get notifications of people sharing the stories that I shared at nine o' clock in the morning when I'm checking my phone at ten o' clock at night. So yeah, switching off doesn't happen, unfortunately.

Similarly, R3 emphasised that:

> I use it all the time. I mean obviously, when you need to focus on a piece of work, when you're writing, it's best not to be checking Twitter every five minutes. You need to concentrate... But no, I don't really have a set pattern and I'm afraid I even do tweet on holiday sometimes. It's just my way of engaging with the world, with a bunch of friends and with other journalists, we're just exchanging information all the time.

Equally, R4 described his pattern of use as constant, but with attempts to disconnect when possible:

> my routine entails that I look at it all the time. I use Tweet Deck for work, so I have multiple feeds open, and that's kind of a big part of my working day and I'm looking at it the whole time. Outside of work, I do look at it fairly regularly because I want to keep up with the news and if, on a Saturday afternoon or a Sunday afternoon or you know, before I go to bed (...)

In similar fashion, most journalists (e.g., R10, R12, R15, R16, R18, R19) mentioned that they consider Twitter addictive in the sense that they feel that they might miss out on important developments. To this end, they also feel that Twitter prolonged their working hours, even though prolonged working hours is part of the journalistic job anyway. For R12, for example, being constantly informed is not only part of her professional identity but also of her personal identity and it finds constant access to information 'reassuring and relaxing'. For R21, this 'addiction to the platform' can be damaging to her professional work as she needs distance from information so as to be able to produce her own content.

Interestingly, with regard to patterns of use, R3 described how Twitter became normalised in his everyday work practices:

(R3). I remember explaining this [the constant engagement with Twitter] to my editor, who was a bit sceptical, I mean long ago. He said, you know, "What are you doing? You're on Twitter all the time, you're wasting your time on it. You should be doing some real work". But the thing is, I was explaining to him, it's not the Twitter that takes the time, it's the links to things that you want to read and to interviews and videos you want to watch. You know, that takes time anyway, I mean, that would take time for whatever kind of journalism you were practicing. Twitter is just a way of finding the bits that you're interested in, the bits where you do actually spend a lot of time. And yeah, like everybody else in journalism, he changed his mind, this editor, because the next time he mentioned Twitter, he said "Do you think you could tweet out this article that we're running this weekend because it's a good one?" Because he recognised that, you know, Twitter was the way to reach an audience.

3.2.6 Normalisation – Theme 3b: The reinforcement of traditional practices and networks

This theme focuses on how news journalists continue to engage with media or political actors. It examines whether Twitter reinforces traditional practices and norms that underwrite the relationships that political actors and news journalists have had in modern times. Specifically, it looks at the traditional reliance on intra-elite sourcing facilitated by Twitter in a way that maintained this form of mutual reliance journalism.

All the journalists interviewed replied that they follow accounts that they consider to be reliable, and accounts that provide quality content, which either means verified information or just intelligent commentary. For this reason, the majority of journalists noted that they primarily follow other journalists first and key political actors second.

For example, R2 noted that he primarily follows news organisations because Twitter is his immediate place for breaking news, unless he gets push notifications from news websites. In addition to that, he follows esteemed journalists, or journalists that have their identities verified, trusted sources and public figures. Similarly, R3 follows other journalists because 'the easiest way of knowing what fellow journalists are up to, is just to follow them on Twitter'. Additionally, R3 follows up to 500 people so he can keep up with the information shared by his contacts, or in his words: 'I want to select the people that provide me with the sort of best value and I choose them'. For R3 humour is one of the qualities he seeks on Twitter so he also follows people who finds interesting or amusing. Even so, for him Twitter is like 'having a bunch of talkative friends in your pocket (...) a wonderful way of communicating at a fairly shallow level with people that you like and find interesting'. R16 takes a similar approach, as for him Twitter's requirement to express laconically means he can find content that it is interesting and funny and also condensed into short messages. For R13, the main criterion is the reliability. Even though she primarily follows other journalists, she only follows those who have proved to be reliable (for instance, in other platforms) or those that she recognises as esteemed figures. For R15, reliability and validity need to be accompanied by continuous flow of content, meaning that he chooses to follow only people that are active in the platform. In addition, R15 referred to Twitter as being populated by journalists, politicians and other influential personalities from media and politics sectors, whose interactions on Twitter affect the news agenda on Twitter and beyond. For this reason, developing a network that includes those actors is seen as beneficial in order to be able to monitor information. For R4, this is particularly important when it is a 'heavy news day' so to aggregate reactions on current developments, either from the audience, politicians, or other journalists and commentators. R8 notes that Twitter is a 'noticeboard for the political community', and for this reason, he sometimes tweets 'in a way that it is perhaps, slightly less understandable to the general audience, knowing that the political audience would get it'. For R3, 'all the information that you have about politics comes through Twitter', which for him is a complete change from the way that journalism was conducted when he started working as journalist in a non-digital era. R4 agrees:

> as someone who follows British politics, if you want to know what's happening in British politics, there is much more information available now than there was thirty, forty years ago when I started being interested. Not solely because of Twitter, but Twitter has sort of prised that open in ways that weren't there before. So I think, if you're an informed user with a capacity to filter out the good stuff

from the bad stuff, it's brilliant because you can access stuff that you would never ever have found or read in a pre-Twitter era.

In other words, and as noted in Chapter 1, journalists' views here support that Twitter reinforces the more traditional practices and mores of news journalism – the reliance on intra-elite sourcing of news and the dominance of official sources by providing a more straightforward and convenient means of access and for cross-checking sources.

3.3 Journalists' evaluation of Twitter's costs and benefits to news journalism

Bringing together the three stages of analysis, this section explores how journalists evaluate Twitter's benefits and costs to news journalism.

3.3.1 Evaluating Twitter's benefits

With regard to Twitter's benefits, immediacy was most journalists' first response. For example, R13, R16, R17 and R18 referred to an unprecedented speed in terms of information seeking and information sharing. To this end, Twitter has benefited journalists' news gathering processes, by giving them access to a wide range of sources and voices. With reference to access to information and to news, R15 compared it to the pre-digital era, when television was always-on the news, which is not necessary anymore, as Twitter offers a better alternative.

Access to information was also linked to access to news sources. R3 noted that through Twitter he has the opportunity to interact with people that he would not have come across otherwise and mentioned that

> Twitter broadened my range of sources, which means that I have been able to talent spot other good journalists, other good sources of information, you know, scientists and political scientists, who are doing good and interesting work are much easier to find nowadays in the Twitter age.

R4 expanded on the benefits of being able to approach experts from various fields, who have already built up their audiences through Twitter, and added:

> For someone like me, that's really useful, because I'm not sure I would have found these people before or even if I knew who was

the academic who was sort of a particular expert on Covid infections or electoral systems or proportional representation or social inequality. To get a comment from them, you'd have to ring them up and try to get it over the phone and now, kind of, they're sort of tweeting away.

(R4)

Furthering this argument, Twitter has made a difference in the pool of people who are in the public space. R4 mentioned the so-called 'legal Twitter' that exists in the United Kingdom's Twittersphere:

> there are some lawyers who basically like being public commentators on law, which was not an option pre-Twitter and now is an option and it means that if you are interested in the legal aspects of any particular political development, there is likely to be a clever person out there who kind of understands it through a lawyer's position, who can give you a view and more often than not, that's worth listening to.

R10 linked immediacy with agenda-setting, as through Twitter's trending topics one has the opportunity 'to feel the society's pulse'. Additionally, it allows journalists to aggregate reactions towards their journalistic work or product, either from the audience, politicians, or other journalists and commentators. This becomes particularly important when it is a 'heavy news day'. For some journalists (R2, R4, R15 and R19), Twitter's affordances make it possible to follow the news in a more systematic way. R15 characterised Twitter's information package as 'perfect' if you know how to use it, as with 'very few interventions you can have a very informative and active sources list'. For R15, this was a process that occurred organically without needing much of her time, as she developed a list of a thousand accounts that she checks occasionally. Others (R2 and R19) use Twitter's app that allows them to separate Twitter's interface into multiple timelines. R19 has divided news sources into national news, international news, analyses and political actors. In each of the lists he includes journalists, news organisations, experts and some ordinary users that have proved to be useful news sources. This systematisation of Twitter use allows him to find news and breaking news in the first instance, and when he needs to investigate, research or understand a topic in depth, he can dive into the analyses.

Likewise, for R4, Twitter facilitated his everyday processes:

I also like being able to use videos and pictures and Twitter is not the only platform for delivering those, but it's a very effective one. Through our blogging technology we can lift and drop the tweeting very very easily, so if someone's been at an event, and they're tweeting, pictures or a video and I know who they are and trust them, then I can share that much more quickly than if you rely on your own cameraman to send you the film and process it.

To this, R21 added that Twitter's idiosyncratic character that obliges users to express themselves laconically encourages journalists to summarise news into a few short messages, even before they publish their work in the outlet they work for. Apart from news gathering, Twitter was seen to have affected positively journalists' self-branding and self-promotion. In the words of R2:

I just primarily use to share the work I've already written. I suppose, from a "brand" point of view, you know, just showcasing what I'm up to and kind of creating that personal brand I suppose off my own account.

For R2, this was partially a personal choice and partially because of his editorial guidelines that encourage journalists to acquire a 'blue tick' (an ID verification process). To this end, he added that:

I have felt a bit more responsibility with Twitter, I've got a blue tick now (...) I feel that has made me want to share it more, because, you know, it's seen by more people and you get a bit more trust than if you don't have one.

R3 referred to 'name recognition', which means that he has his own 'personal platform' that he did not have before Twitter, at least to the same extent. Even though he was familiar with blogs that were a more immediate way of communicating with people, he considered them to be less important than Twitter as 'they did not attract huge audiences, whereas Twitter is much more visible'. According to R5, when one considers this in relation to Twitter's affordances (for instance the 'retweet' function), the benefits could be really significant:

I share some of the work I am really proud of. And then, all it takes is one person with like several hundred thousand followers or a million followers to retweet it. And you get tons and tons of people seeing your article. And then there are tons more clicks, tons more revenue, tons more engagement. Just like one good retweet on Twitter from like a really big, big, high-profile account can improve a story's performance enormously.

3.3.2 Evaluating Twitter's costs

The most prominent response concerned the 'diffused toxicity in the platform' (R1). R16 referred to a 'systematic degradation of public discourse' and used the metaphor of the 'Roman arena' to describe the conditions in the platform that 'breed the vulgarity of human instincts that lead people to be indulged in sharing unverified views'. In a way, he feels that Twitter encourages a form of aggressiveness that leads to the reduction of political discourse into slogans. Toxicity is also linked to abuse, which could also be unprovoked. As R16 notes, 'I can even post a full stop on Twitter and there will be people that will attack me. Just because they can and they know they can reach me'. R1 and R17 consider anonymity as the main cause, as people hide behind the anonymity Provided. However, R17 pointed out that there are known journalistic or political accounts that are toxic as well. R3 noted that it enables 'people who don't like you or just want to sound off or tell you how rubbish you are to do that anonymously and easily'.

For R8, the main reason abuse happens is the immediacy of the platform as she thinks that 'people wouldn't do [these abusive comments] if they meet you in the street'. In agreement, R19 also considered Twitter's instantaneity as a primary cause for abuse and referred to the feeling of 'instant reaction' that Twitter creates, that makes everyone hurry to reach conclusions or to set their minds on a specific opinion. For R19, this is the case for journalists too, as on Twitter they feel they need to take a side on every single topic and to be part of every single conversation.

R3 highlighted that abuse is more frequent towards women journalists, and that it became more common when the platform was normalised. In his words:

> I recognise that for some people, Twitter is just horrible and there's no way of dealing with that. I do remember that in the early days, Twitter was a really pleasant environment. I mean, I think this happened with all these forms of communication on the Internet. In the early days of blogging, it was a small world mostly, you followed people you knew, you engaged with people you knew

and you had interesting conversations. And then, of course, you know, as it grew bigger, more people piled in with the negatives, and the same thing happened with Twitter (R3).

Some journalists discussed their coping mechanisms towards the toxicity that exists in the platform.

Disengaging, disconnecting, using Twitter narrowly, and even self-censoring are some of them. R16, an active user of the platform, concluded that he would not mind if Twitter disappeared tomorrow, as this would solve his dilemma of whether he should disconnect from the platform. Likewise, R3 pointed out that:

> I engage much less than I used to on Twitter as a place for discussion, because, yeah, life's too short to get into unpleasant conversations with people who just want to tell you that they dislike you. I mean, it's less of an issue for me, because I'm a man, not a woman, I am white, I do news rather than commentary... I know that there are lots of people who get it far, far worse on Twitter, but still, I get enough abuse there to think it's not a pleasant place to spend too long.
>
> (R3)

The choice to be connected or disconnected occurs both subconsciously and not strategically, but also consciously – as R8 said:

> I don't use Twitter to engage in too much dialogue. Because I think the danger is you end up maybe treating it like a private e-mail exchange, when it is actually a public thing. I am very conscious of the fact that Twitter is another form of broadcasting, the Twitter I have is through the BBC, and therefore I need to be very responsible about what I am tweeting on it.

R9 added that she avoids any personal use of the platform, to minimise chances of receiving disrespectful comments, whereas R7 framed this avoidance to engage in terms of his perceived or imagined audience:

> I think that one of the things that I have become actually conscious of is that one of the risks when you are engaging on Twitter is that you have to be careful, to make sure that you continue to write for yourself and not write for or around any perceived audience and in particular any particular perceived Twitter audience. There is a danger that you can find yourself writing things with the

thought of how your article would be perceived by the sort of the Twitter community and how you will have to defend and represent your article to the Twitter community.

(R7)

R3, on the other hand, chose not to disconnect, but to 'mute negativity and toxicity out' by muting many accounts when this becomes overwhelming. Even though he sometimes is intentionally provocative because he enjoys the dialogue, he recognises that 'when it becomes overwhelming it feels negative (...) for some people. Twitter is just absolutely horrible and there's no way of dealing with that'. R21 added that this is a trap and she noted that there are many times that she spends a lot of time considering whether she would write something on Twitter. However, she mentioned that she tries to avoid the temptation of self-censoring as this is 'the aim of the people that attack journalists'.

R9 added that toxicity was already present in online newspapers' comment sections, as 'the relationship with the audience really changed when their newspaper column migrated online and people had the chance to comment in the respective section', and emphasised that it is of outmost importance to not pay too much attention to abusive comments, as whomever does that 'can end up slightly drowning beneath the sea of it, sometimes'. In similar vein, R5 pointed out that 'you can be on Twitter for a long time and it can be very depressing or very bleak or to feel that it is a relentless day of very depressing news. So, sometimes you can be like, okay, I've just got to switch off now'. For R5, it is important for journalists to protect their mental health, and a way to do that is to know when to switch off. In his words:

> if you get too lost in a rabbit hole of just scrolling through those comments it can really just take a hit on your mental state (...) I've learned as hard as it is to try not to get lost in the comments and replies on Twitter because it can just be just grim basically.

For R6, the responsibility lies to some extend with the audiences, as audiences occasionally cannot separate reporting from the endorsement of an opinion, stressing that 'reporting a fact is not the same as agreeing with the facts'. Thinking that is misleading and feeds abusive behaviours. In agreement, R12 added that it is very important 'to train the audiences to be able to discern fact from fiction as this would have a great effect on their reactions'. For R21, the responsibility also lies with the platform that does not impose clear rules. Even though 'putting in place a sort of unofficial (or almost unofficial) rules and restrictions of what people can and cannot say, what opinions can or cannot hold, and how they express them can be dangerous and all of us have to be aware of and have to be careful' (R7), R21 argued that Twitter can simply ask people to verify their identities, as this would massively enhance the platform's quality. It would also prevent people from attacking or threatening journalists.

For R15, toxicity and abuse occur when too many people are involved in the conversation or in the dissemination of information, as it becomes inevitable that information and public discourse get distorted. Apart from Twitter occasionally turning into a toxic environment for journalists, interviewees added some other aspects that could be seen as Twitter's negatively affecting news journalism. R2 and R21, for example, mentioned the diffusion of disinformation as a significant cause for concern. R21 referred to many instances where journalists are tempted to tweet a story really quickly without fully verifying all facts. However, for R21, this situation feeds a vicious circle: when journalists share unverified information, they become targets of toxicity and abuse, which then leads to self-censorship. R19 frames this distortion as 'noise' that is quite prevalent on Twitter, also because there are not any specific rules and conditions to prevent this. For R16, this 'noise' can be misleading as 'Twitter is falsely seen by journalists as representing society, which is not the case'. For R17, the real issue is that people become very defensive about their views and 'it becomes almost impossible to correct a false view, even if you try to do so by being extremely polite'.

Information disorder though does not occur only because of the diffusion of disinformation but also due to the difficulty journalists may have to maintain a pluralistic timeline. R2 noted that 'I think the issue with Twitter is, you only get from it the views of the people that you follow. It's very hard to have a balanced timeline, I think, so it can often skew your reaction to particular stories'. For this reason, for R2, gathering news or aggregating reactions on Twitter is not a straightforward choice, adding that:

> I think it can send you into a false sense of security about people's views (…) I think it's a danger of not showcasing a general view of people's reactions to events, but more of the people that you follow and their ideas. Obviously, it really is just down to who you follow, which I think from a journalist's perspective can be slightly dangerous (…) I might use it for trending content, it's handy to see what people are talking about and what's gaining traction. But I think

it's too skewed, with different, sort of, polarizing views but you're obviously one of those, which is the group of people you follow.

R11 considered 'truth-seeking' on Twitter exceptionally difficult and time-consuming even for journalists who are professionals and are trained to do so, as this could be a journalist's 'whole working day'. On a different note, R4 referred to the financial effects that Twitter may have on news journalism as a business, pointing out that:

> Twitter is a competitor medium to news websites and if people are feeling that they can get all their news just by reading their Twitter feed without actually clicking on any of the links and looking at them in more detail, then that's a problem for the industry more widely, because, Twitter don't pay me for my tweets, my newspaper does.

Interestingly, through all interviews, Twitter's negative effect on news journalism was juxtaposed with its positive effects, as a way to maintain a balanced approach. To this end, R3 was optimistic:

> I don't agree with the negative interpretation of Twitter on that. I mean, I think the thing about Twitter is that it's faster, so disinformation can spread more quickly, but the rebuttal of disinformation can also spread more quickly. I may be sort of madly optimistic, but I just think that the Internet generally is progress and I think it is leading to greater understanding. I mean, I know that there're problems with polarisation and arguments and abuse and all that, but misinformation, I think, can be killed more quickly on the Internet now.

4 From disruption to normalisation
Journalists' accounts on Twitter (2009–2021)

Baumgartner and Jones (2009), who adapted the theory of punctuated equilibrium to enable them to assess the impact of various forms of social policy, came to the methodological conclusion that longitudinal studies are the most appropriate types of empirical research to understand and evaluate the impact of punctuated equilibrium. Following them and to properly account for the evolution of Twitter usage in news journalism, we need to understand how professional journalists have used Twitter and the ways this use has potentially altered news journalism itself. To this end, 27 Twitter accounts belonging to professional journalists from Greece and the United Kingdom, over the period of 2009–2021 were studied. The aim of the study was to identify and track the three stages of punctuated equilibrium.

Overall, the findings pointed to the following evolutionary timelines:

1 For account activity: (a) short-term disruption 2009–2012; (b) short-term adaption 2012–2017; and (c) mid- to long-term normalisation 2017–2021.
2 For the use of hashtags: (a) short-term disruption 2009–2011; (b) short-term adaption 2012–2016; and (c) mid- to long-term normalisation 2017–2021.
3 For the use of mentions: (a) short-term disruption 2009–2012; (b) short-term adaption 2012–2017; and (c) mid- to long-term normalisation 2017–2021.

One important point here is that 2009 was chosen as a starting point because this was when Twitter shifted from a 'friend-oriented' platform to a 'news-oriented' one. In 2009, the prompt 'What are you doing?' was replaced by 'What is happening?' This simple (and elegant) change in Twitter's purpose from descriptive self-centredness to an outward facing reporting of events signified a changed from Twitter as 'more of an information network than a social one' (Burgess & Baym, 2020, p. 12). This subsequently changed the character of the uses of Twitter by its users in a subtle but fundamental way – it quite simply shifted the communicative purposes of the platform (Burgess & Baym, 2020, p. 34). The new purpose of Twitter was to enable individuals to report events as they affected 'me' or, in so far as 'I' was able to and for 'me' to account for those events 'I' witnessed. It was only a very short step for this to be interpolated into news journalism – which it duly was.

The news journalists selected for the study were chosen on the basis of their accounts' popularity, measured by the number of their followers.[1] For the U.K. journalists, the basis was 100.000 followers, whereas for Greek journalists the figure reduced to 50.000 followers.[2] The final sample includes 27 journalists, 12 from Greece and 15 from the United Kingdom. Male journalists accounted for 70% and female journalists for 30% of the sample. In terms of their specific job description, 27% self-identified as columnists, 27% as editors, 19% as presenters, 15% as journalists, 8% as correspondents, and 4% as filmmakers. The chapter begins with an account of the participants, progresses to examine the participants' first tweets, it demonstrates how they present their biography on the platform, and finally discusses their use of the platform.

4.1 An account of the participants

Table 4.1 presents participants' work profile, gender and number of followers.

From the selected journalists, 59% joined Twitter in 2009 and 26% joined Twitter in 2011. 7% joined in 2010 and 4% in 2012. A small percentage (4%) joined Twitter in 2008; however, they did not use their account during that year.

4.2 The participants' first Tweets: 2009–2011

37% of participants posted their first tweet in 2009; 22% in 2010, 37% in 2011 and 4% in 2013. All of their first tweets reveal a natural initial awkwardness on how to approach the platform and an uncertainty about Twitter's requirements, benefits and costs. In some cases, this awkwardness is expressed explicitly, or implicitly in terms of the communicative strategies employed, for example when they post a link without any explanation, or their textual choices, for example choosing not to follow grammatical or syntactical rules (see some indicative examples on Table 4.2).

Table 4.1 Participants' work profile, gender and followers

Name	Media organisation	Position	Gender	Twitter account	Number of followers (April 2022)
Antonopoulou, Eva	*SKAI*	Journalist Presenter	Female	@eantonopoulou	73.2K
Cadwalladr, Carole	*The Guardian* *The Observer*	Writer	Female	@carolecadwall	712.6K
Chatzinikolaou, Nikos	*Realnews* *Real.gr* *Enikos.gr*	Editor	Male	@NChatzinikolaou	638.7K
Chatzistefanou, Aris	Freelancer	Journalist Filmmaker	Male	@xstefanou	70.1K
Danezis, Sotiris	Freelancer	War Correspondent News Presenter Documentary Filmmaker	Male	@SotirisDanezis	84.9K
Denaxa, Maria	*Star TV,* *Real Group*	Foreign correspondent	Female	@mdenaxa	68.2K
Evagelatos, Nikos	*Mega TV* *NewsIT*	Presenter	Male	@NikosEvagelatos	65.7K
Goodall, Lewis	*BBC*	Editor	Male	@lewis_goodall	264.9K
Hodges, Dan	*The Mail on Sunday*	Commentator	Male	@DPJHodges	164K
Hyde, Marina	*The Guardian*	Columnist	Female	@MarinaHyde	474.9K
Islam, Faisal	*BBC*	Editor	Male	@faisalislam	372.3K
Kuenssberg, Laura	*BBC*	Political Editor	Female	@bbclaurak	1.3M
Maguire, Kevin	*Daily Mirror* *New Statesman* *GMB*	Associate Editor, Columnist, Commentator	Male	@Kevin_Maguire	304.4K

(Continued)

Name	Media organisation	Position	Gender	Twitter account	Number of followers (April 2022)
Maitlis, Emily	BBC	Presenter News anchor	Female	@maitlis	467.2K
Nelson, Fraser	The Spectator The Telegraph	Editor, Columnist	Male	@FraserNelson	284.6K
Oikonomou, Dimitris	SKAI	Journalist	Male	@dimoikonomu	85.4K
Portosalte, Aris	SKAI	Journalist	Male	@ArisPortosalte	156.3K
Rawnsley, Andrew	The Guardian The Observer	Chief political commentator	Male	@andrewrawnsley	408.2K
Rentoul, John	The Independent	Chief political commentator	Male	@JohnRentoul	149.8K
Rigby, Beth	Sky News	Political Editor Presenter	Female	@BethRigby	386.7K
Robinson, Nick	BBC	Presenter	Male	@bbcnickrobinson	1M
Sroiter, Antonis	ALPHA	Presenter	Male	@AntonisSroiter	50.4K
Tsapanidou, Popi	iPop	Journalist	Female	@tsapanidou	621.7K
Vaxevanis, Kostas	Kouti Pandoras Documento	Journalist Publisher Editor	Male	@KostasVaxevanis	494.5K
Waterson, Jim	The Guardian	Editor	Male	@jimwaterson	258.2K
Waugh, Paul	The i Paper BBC	Chief Political Commentator Presenter	Male	@paulwaugh	214K
Xaritatos, Spiros	Propago	Journalist	Male	@SpirosXaritatos	69.9K

Table 4.2 Explicit awkwardness in first tweets[3]

Name	First tweet
Antonopoulou, Eva	(1) discovering ALSO twitter....! Hello......
Chatzinikolaou Nikos	(1) I am going for news broadcasting and tv-show. We will talk later. Happy to find you. (2) The friend who wrote that I came for ... reading is right! (3) The egg is fine! I have not yet hatched my egg at your court yet ... See you later.
Chatzistefanou, Aris	http://www.xstefanou.com (1) Editing next doc "Morpheous Nightmare"
Denaxa, Maria	(1) @YanniKouts bonjour maintenant ;O) (2) http://t.co/XQif206
Evagelatos, Nikos	(1) Hello to everyone
Goodall, Lewis	(1) I came. I saw. I tweeted.
Hyde, Marina	(1) @username I'm so technologically quarterwitted I have never even been on Facebook, so picture will come in due course. BABY STEPS.
Islam, Faisal	(1) Econotweeting
Kuenssberg, Laura	(1) hello - thanks for following! -tweets start from TUC in sept...
Maitlis, Emily	(1) Newsnight (2) question time (3) i am the slowest person in the twitter class. and have three people helping me. is this normal?
Nelson, Fraser	(1) Inaugural tweet - test.
Oikonomou, Dimitris	(1) First Responder - golema.gr http://t.co/ISet6su via @golemagr (2) You have gone crazy with Twitter I am counting your posts as if I am counting sheep so as to fall asleep
Portosalte, Aris	(1) Guys I joined abruptly, thanks for the welcoming...it's me!!!!!!!
Rawnsley, Andrew	(1) Reviewed Lance Price's book about PMs vs media for Sun's Obs. Cracking read. If you like that, you may like this. http://twitpic.com/11bi6k
Rentoul, John	(1) One quarter of Tesco sales go through self-service checkouts. Other people are more 21st century than me.
Sroiter, Antonis	(1) 'Antonis Sroiter first tweet' says here.. Okay..I am joining Twitter's 'home' feeling a bit awkward. (2) As if you are going home to meet your future wife's dad, having gifts in your hands. What do you say to break the ice? (3) Well, hello, nice weather today!!

(Continued)

Name	First tweet
Tsapanidou, Popi	(1) @username just joined and try to figure it our...John! Hello. I am looking how many familiar people are here. You are one of them.
Waugh, Paul	(1) @iaindale Many thanks for your kind words. Slowly getting the hang of this thang! (2) @timmontgomerie Many thanks for your generous tweet. Feel like I'm on a big learning curve on this thing! (3) Woah! Inundated with followers - hello to you all. Hope to bring you the latest gossip, news and comment from Westminster in real time.
Xaritatos, Spiros	(1) ...looking for GM on the road to Rythmos Party!

In Chapter 3, the disruptive impact of Twitter on news journalism was described through the way it affected news cycles, news sourcing, news gathering, and the nature of the interviewed journalists' engagement with their audience and Twitter's inherent toxicity. These issues were not something our participants reflected on in their first encounters with the platform. Rather in these first tweets, the tone is one of enthusiasm, humour and self-deprecation. In some cases, a display of neonate skilful use. In essence, there is a pre-disruptive sense of optimism and expectation.

These first tweets quickly evolved into the requirement to present oneself to the audience, to don a Twitter identity and to display mastery of a new technology. In brief, the first disruptive event that the participants faced was the choices about how to present themselves on the platform and how to demonstrate their skills. It is therefore helpful to see how news journalists adjusted to and normalised the use of Twitter in and through the task of introducing themselves to their audiences.

4.3 The 'presentation of self': how the participants chose to display their biographical information

Twitter enables users to provide their biographical information in more or less any manner, as there are no specific guidelines. Sometimes this information is presented whimsically, factually, obscurely and so on. For the study's participants, it provided an opportunity to present biographical information in the form of what Ottovordemgentschenfelde (2017, p. 76) refers to as a 'digital business card'. These business cards allow journalists to choose how they present themselves to their audiences and constitute the first impression Twitter users get of a journalist's account. Analysing these business cards allows us to examine how our participants wished to engage with their audience and upon what basis (formal or informal) in the first instance. The different types of information included in journalists' digital cards was analysed by Hedman (2020, p. 677) as a form of self-presentation in the platform which consisted of four basic attributes: (a) personal name – a chosen form of identification, (b) profession – professional title or description, (c) contact information – a web link (URL) as well as personal information such as references to their personal interests or family, and (d) a disclaimer – usually in the form of 'views are my own and not my employer's' or 'retweets are not endorsements'. Using these four attributes, Table 4.3 presents the different versions of self-presentation adopted by the participants.[4]

To take the four attributes in turn. In the selected sample, all journalists provide their personal name in full (both first and second name); no one used initials or titles. 74% include their profession. In this category, some journalists include their specific job title (for example, foreign correspondent, policy editor, columnist and chief political commentator), and details about the medium they work for. The majority of journalists use neutral tone to describe their professional status. Exception to this rule is Andrew Rawnsley, who enhances his self-presentation by explicitly referring to his professional achievements: 'The Observer's award-winning Chief Political Commentator, critically-acclaimed broadcaster and author of Number One bestseller, The End of the Party'. Only a minority of journalists (26%) included contact information in their self-description, such as their email address or links to their other social media channels (e.g., Instagram). Even so, 41% of journalists include a link (URL) to an external website, which includes their professional profile, or their publications. Lastly, only 22% of journalists include a personal comment, usually a humorous one, compared to 59% that prefer to not include any personal information. There is though, a small percentage of journalists (19%) that use this space to advertise a book that they have published. No one issued a disclaimer of any kind.

This presentation of the self through the 'digital business cards' was part of a commonplace disruptive process that, as noted above, demanded from journalists that they now had to adjust to the requirements of presenting themselves to different audiences on Twitter by adhering to Twitter's concision requirement, meaning then that this self-presentation needs to be no longer than 160 characters.[5] For all 27 journalists, this meant engaging in some kind of informal style of

Table 4.3 Journalists' self-presentation on Twitter

Name	Personal name	Profession	Contact information	Disclaimer	Personal information
Antonopoulou, Eva	Yes	Yes Journalist	Yes Instagram Facebook	No	No
Cadwalladr, Carole	Yes	Yes Guardian & Observer writer	No Only URL to external professional staff website	No	Yes Founder of organisations, Comments: 'Late adopter', 'Late giver-upper'
Chatzistefanou, Aris	Yes	Yes Journalist	No Only URL to external professional project website	No	No
Chatzinikolaou, Nikos	Yes	Yes Editor	No Only URL to external professional publication website	No	No
Danezis, Sotiris	Yes	Yes Documentary Producer, War Correspondent, News Anchor	No Only URL to YouTube channel	No	Yes Comment: 'Biased against violence & injustice'
Denaxa, Maria	Yes	Yes Foreign correspondent	Yes Email	Yes 'All views expressed solely mine'	No

Name		Role		
Evagelatos, Nikos	Yes	No	No Only URL to external professional publication website	No
Goodall, Lewis	Yes	Yes Policy Editor	Yes Email Instagram	No Book advert
Hodges, Dan	Yes	Yes Commentator	No	Yes Soundbites: 'Worst political pundit in the West' and 'Clown Prince' Comments: 'Didn't attend private school' and 'Mingled with Tories'
Hyde, Marina	Yes	Yes Guardian columnist	No Only URL to external professional staff website	No
Islam, Faisal	Yes	Yes Economics Editor	No	No Book advert
Kuenssberg, Laura	Yes	Yes	No Only URL to external professional staff website	No
Maguire, Kevin	Yes	Yes Associate editor Columnist Commentator Visiting professor	No	Yes 'Northerner in the South'

(*Continued*)

Name	Personal name	Profession	Contact information	Disclaimer	Personal information
Maitlis, Emily	No	Yes Presenter	No	No	Yes Founder of organisations Comment: 'Appalling typing'
Nelson, Fraser	Yes	Yes Editor Columnist	No	No	No Board member in organisations
Oikonomou, Dimitris	Yes	No	No	No	No
Portosalte, Aris	Yes	No	No	No	No
Rawnsley, Andrew	Yes	Yes Chief Political Commentator, Broadcaster Author	Only URL to external professional staff website	No	Book advert
Rentoul, John	Yes	Yes Chief political commentator Visiting professor Author	Only URL to external professional staff website	No	No Book advert
Rigby, Beth	Yes	Yes Political Editor	No Only URL to external professional publication website	No	No
Robinson, Nick	Yes	Yes Presenter Author Former BBC/ITV political editor	No Only URL to external professional publication website	No	No Book advert

From disruption to normalisation: journalists' Twitter accounts   85

Name	Col2	Col3	Col4	Col5
Sroiter, Antonis	Yes	No	No	Yes Comment: 'Candidate to live in planet Zeus where day has exactly 3,450 hours. There I will be able to catch up with everything'
Tsapanidou, Popi	Yes	No	Yes Instagram Facebook	No
Vaxevanis, Kostas	Yes	No	Yes Instagram	No
Waterson, Jim	Yes	Yes Media editor	Yes Open DMs Email Only URL to external professional publication website	No
Waugh, Paul	Yes	Yes Chief political commentator	No	No
Xaritatos, Spiros	Yes	Yes Mediator certified by the Ministry of Justice Lawyer Journalist	Yes Instagram	No

constant technological 're-skilling' or 'up-skilling' so as to meet the different demands (informal and formal) imposed upon them by news organisations and peer pressure with regard to the presentation of their biographical information. From this early form of disruption to the end of the study in 2021, it is evident that most journalists had adapted and normalised their self-presentation on Twitter (Table 4.3).

The new norm consisted of: presenting themselves first, in their professional capacity, and by explicitly referring to their specific job title. Second, by attempting to brand themselves by 'commodifying their online persona' and 'to tie their audience to themselves rather than their employees' (Maares et al., 2020, p. 4), a tendency that has been become more and more widely accepted (Hedman, 2020; Mellado & Hermida, 2021) for example by the use of a link to their professional website (their staff profile and/or their publications' website), or by the inclusion of a snippet of promotion, such as an advertisement to their published work (usually, a book they authored). Third, by not including any personal information (see Chapter 3, *Personal Touch*). Here the vast majority of the interviewees expressed their scepticism and hesitation in exposing aspects of their personal life on Twitter preferring to 'humanise' their professional persona through humorous asides or commentary, insights into their nature or ironic comments directed at people they were reporting on. What is revealed by the study is that the demand for self-presentation, as a form of audience engagement, had little disruptive impact on what or how they went about their job. Professional distance was maintained, appropriateness used as a guideline and boundaries of civility were observed. Such disruption as there was and which was prompted by Twitter (see below) did not occur in and through the requirements of digital self-presentation – in other words, our participating news journalists did not become 'friends' or 'colleagues' with audiences through the use of Twitter based familiarity or using Twitter as 'getting to know you.'

4.4 Account core features: account activity, use of hashtags and mentions and formatting tweets and textual choices

Moving on from self-presentations is the inescapable (and more revealing) form of presentation that occurs structurally and inevitably through the way news journalists use Twitter. This is through their accounts, which are information profiles of what is regarded as important. The way journalists handle their Twitter accounts represents the ways through which we can assess how news journalism

From disruption to normalisation: journalists' Twitter accounts 87

Table 4.4 Account core features

Account core features	Account features (from disruption to normalisation, 2009–2021)
Activity (4.3.1)	Level of activity on Twitter Indicating level of journalists' engagement with the platform over time.
Hashtags and mentions (4.3.2)	Use of hashtags and mentions Indicating level of journalists' engagement with the platform and with other users over time.
Formatting of tweets and textual choices (4.3.3)	Structure of tweets and elements of tonality, formality, emotionality Indicating journalists' communicative techniques on Twitter.

was affected by Twitter. In order to properly understand this, we need to look at the essential and core features of the participants' Twitter accounts – namely account activity, the use of hashtags and mentions and finally, the formatting of the tweets (Table 4.4). Each of these core features follows an evolutionary pattern of usage described below.

To take the account core features in the order of Table 4.4, the analysis of the activity of the accounts is a quantitative feature that enhances our understanding of journalists' initial engagement with Twitter over time. The analysis of journalists' use of hashtags and mentions allows us understand how Twitter is used interactionally, as 'part of the grammar for understanding different uses of Twitter' and as affordances that 'ultimately came to drive the datafied, metricized, newsy, promotional platform' that Twitter is today (Burgess & Baym, 2020, p. 33). Finally, the analysis of formatting tweets and textual choices highlights the participants various communication techniques within the platform.

4.4.1 Account activity

The activity of each account reflects the degree the platform is integrated into journalists' work routines and the extent to which Twitter is part of their everyday journalistic practices. From the participant journalists in the study, John Rentoul and Dan Hodges are the most active Twitter users, whereas the least active are Jim Waterson and Antonis Sroiter. However, this is not an indicator of popularity, as

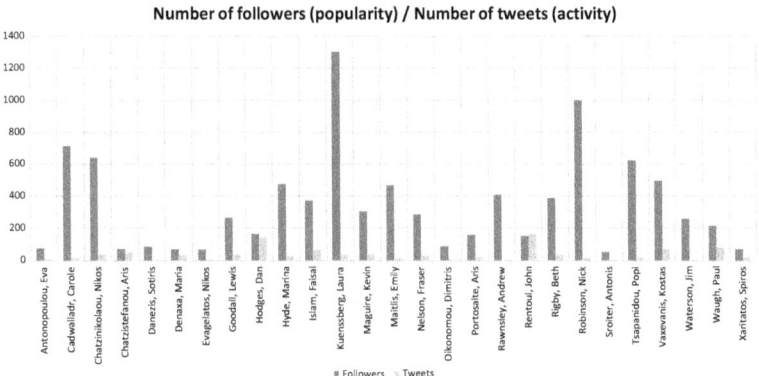

Figure 4.1 Journalists' popularity versus journalists' activity on Twitter.

in some cases, journalists' popularity on Twitter is not dependent on their activity within the platform (Figure 4.1), but by other, exogenous factors, such as their brand, visibility and the extent to which they appear in other news channels. This accords with the view that Twitter is part of a wider media ecosystem, in which Twitter news journalists exist and work. Building a 'followership' that extends beyond Twitter is proof of the interconnectedness within such an ecosystem but within the confines of Twitter alone it does not point to large numbers defining news agendas or how things are reported. Where large numbers influence action requires a form of presence greater than the one which Twitter caters for by itself and in isolation of other platforms.

Additionally, the no-correlation between activity and popularity may disguise activity elsewhere. As Madianou and Miller (2011) note, none of the social media platforms can be properly understood if considered in isolation, since each platform acquires meaning through its relation to other platforms. The authors describe a complexity that highlights an 'inextricable link' between online platforms, but also between them and social structures (Van Dijck et al., 2018, p. 2). Madianou and Miller (2011) suggest that journalists reside in a 'polymedia ecosystem' where inter-platform activity better accounts for the level of account activity. Needless to say, this polymedia approach was not taken in this study. Even so, to posit that news journalists exist in a media ecosystem or a 'polymedia' setting suggests an interconnectedness between multiple platforms that has become normalised.

In terms of the evolutionary approach (Figure 4.2), all accounts present a distinct pattern that is characterised by a slow start, a peak

From disruption to normalisation: journalists' Twitter accounts 89

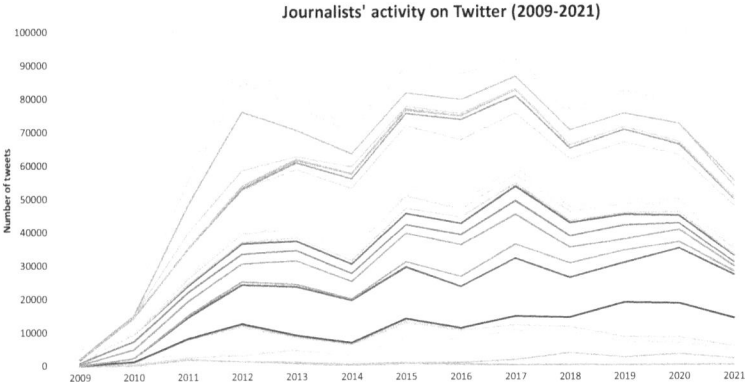

Figure 4.2 Journalists' activity on Twitter (2009–2021).

of activity and a decline, even though, the timeframes for each journalist are different. Considering this pattern through the lens of punctuated equilibrium theory allows us to divide this activity into the three stages of short-term disruption, short-term adaption and mid- to long-term normalisation. These stages allow us to analyse how Twitter's disruptive presence evolved: that is, how this disruptive force was initially experienced, how it subsequently spread and whether it escalated or was adapted to (Vollmer, 2013, p. 14) and finally how it was absorbed and normalised. The evolutionary pattern that accounts' activity revealed was[6]:

1. Short-term disruption (2009–2012): the period before activity on the platform reaches its peak;
2. Short-term adaption (2012–2017): the period of activity after the platform reaches its peak; and
3. Mid- to long-term normalisation (2017–2021): the period of activity which includes activity on the platform after its final peak and in accordance with journalists' own definitions of what practices constitute 'normal and routine use'.

The majority of the participants in the study joined Twitter in 2009, even though during this year they posted very few tweets on the platform. Their activity starts to increase in 2010 and 2011 and reaches a first peak in 2012. In years 2013 and 2014, there is a decline that leads to another peak in years 2016 and 2017. After 2017, there is a decline in most journalists' use of the platform, which is particularly evident in years 2020 and 2021. The evolutionary pattern (Figure 4.2) reinforces the argument that change is typically a steady and normal state, punctuated by commonplace disruptions as described in Chapter 2. The many disruptions that news journalists were confronted with were commonplace which attracted little notice beyond the confines of news organisations. Only certain types of disruptions which displace traditional values and practices can be regarded as special and then only when they are seen to affect people who are not directly involved in the displacement itself. The commonplace disruptions that our participating news journalists experienced revealed the fact that account activity was quickly normalised and stabilised because it was maintained by the existing structures within the institutions that saw accounts as an 'additional tool' that facilitated certain pre-existing processes and relationships.

What the accounts' activity evolutionary pattern reveals is that for most of the participant journalists there was a slow start in joining Twitter, which suggest that during the period (2009–2012) there was no 'shock of the new' form of disruption as a form of a displacement kind. By 2012, evolutionary adaption was undertaken as a form of accommodation of new forms of adjustment on how to utilise an account. This lasted from 2012–2017. During this period journalists developed their coping strategies in dealing with Twitter: as we have seen in Chapter 2 and 3 for some, they adopted a strategy of resistance that revealed a decline in the use of Twitter 2009–2021. For the pragmatics, what is revealed is gradual stabilisation of use 2017–2021, while for the enthusiastic adopters of Twitter periodic stabilisation and then new peaks of activity during the whole period (2009–2021). Clearly not every journalist felt comfortable using Twitter or that it was necessary to maintain a very active presence on Twitter. The perception of Twitter as an extension of journalists' digital toolkit (Chapter 3) suggests the routinisation of the previously 'new' and the normalisation of Twitter as part of their everyday journalistic routines. Indeed, after 2019 a decline in Twitter activity is discernible.

Both peaks and declines are explained by punctuated equilibrium. Baumgartner and Jones (2009, p. 6) point out that evolutionary patterns are directly affected by positive or negative feedback at any point in time. To this end, they argue that 'when a system is subject to negative feedback, an initial disturbance becomes smaller as it works its way through time. In positive feedback, small disturbances become amplified, causing major disruptions as they operate across time'. Similarly, they add 'disruptions or shocks are absorbed and counteracted by opposing forces, and all understand that the system will remain in place: negative feedback dominates and stability ensues' (2009, p. 288). Therefore, the decline in activity after 2019 might be related to negative feedback (here, journalists' perceptions of Twitter's costs) – which in Twitter's case concerns toxicity.

The year with the highest level of activity on Twitter differs among journalists, however, for most journalists that participated in the study, the years 2012 and 2017 witnessed journalists' greatest uses of Twitter. This suggests that the main points of adaption for most journalists was either 2012 or 2017. The level of use of Twitter and the activity on the platform appear to conform to the process of increasing normalisation. The analysis through the stages of punctuated equilibrium enables us to reject ideas that suggest that these moments (such as the aforementioned peaks) act as single moments of radical transformations – rather, they are peaks that indicate the move to the next stage, here that of short-term adaption.

4.4.2 Use of hashtags and mentions

Hashtags and mentions form another of Twitter's core features, each of which are the primary technological expressions of Twitter's version of sociality in general and for journalists their professional sociality in particular. These two features are central to users' ability to connect, 'weaving the idiosyncratic micro syntax' of the medium (the limited number of characters used in a tweet) 'into the fabric of sociality' (Van Dijck, 2013, p. 72). In addition, they transformed Twitter into the most interactive platform with regard to news (Bruns, 2018, p. 9), fostering social listening and professional dialogue and enabling a new form of public relations (Burgess & Baym, 2020). At the same time, they made cultural participation, human communication, and social connection calculable through processes of datafication[7] (Burgess & Baym, 2020, p. 34).

Each of these features was proposed by users in 2006 and 2007, and was initially user-driven, before the platform fully incorporated them into their practices, as their primary affordances. As Papacharissi (2014, p. 34) notes in relation to hashtags, 'they emerged organically as a way for users to organise their conversations thematically before those conventions were formally incorporated into Twitter's infrastructure. The hashtag is a brief keyword or abbreviation prefixed with the symbol '#', and it emerged out of the need 'to coordinate Twitter activity as the flow of tweets started to grow beyond an easily manageable size' (Burgess & Baym, 2020, p. 65). The goal of this feature is to allow users to conduct dialogue concerning a particular subject, by feeding commentary into a particular stream, thus it is useful for coordinating conversations on Twitter. In addition, Twitter users include the hashtag to enhance the dissemination of a tweet by categorising it under a specific theme. In other words, it enhances the visibility of a tweet. Twitter turned the hashtag into a 'highly significant, multifunctional feature' (Burgess & Baym, 2020, p. 61). Overall, the study revealed three different styles of use with regard to hashtags inserted by news journalists. The first is the 'dialogical', essentially by using the hashtag to feed a commentary into a particular stream. The second is the 'official', that is accepting keywords that were widely accepted by Twitter users in relation to a particular theme. And the third is promotional, that is used to promote journalists' work in various platforms.

Figure 4.3 shows journalists' usage of hashtags compared to their total number of tweets for the examined timeframe (2009–2021), which moves towards a tendency to use hashtags only minimally. A finding that echoes previous research which also shows very limited use of this feature equally by media organisations (legacy and net-native) as well as by journalists in Greece and the United Kingdom (Dagoula, 2017, 2019).

From an evolutionary point of view, the use of hashtags by news journalists presents a distinct pattern, similar to journalists' activity in the platform. As with journalists' activity over time, the use of personal hashtags reveals a slow start, a peak of activity and a decline.

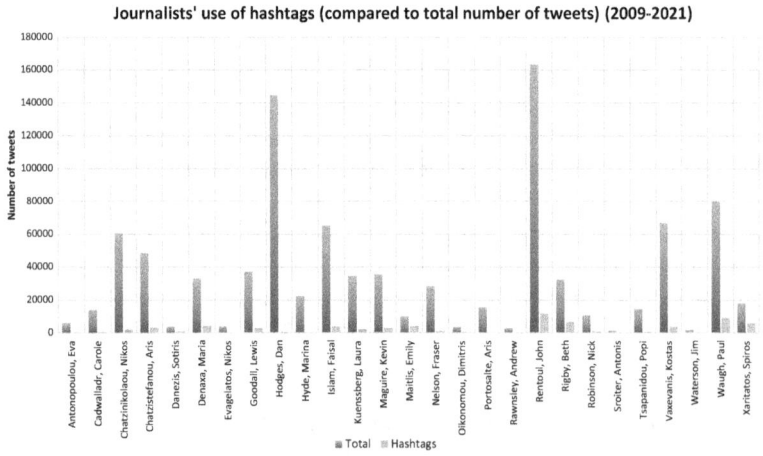

Figure 4.3 Journalists' use of hashtags compared to total number of tweets (2009–2021).

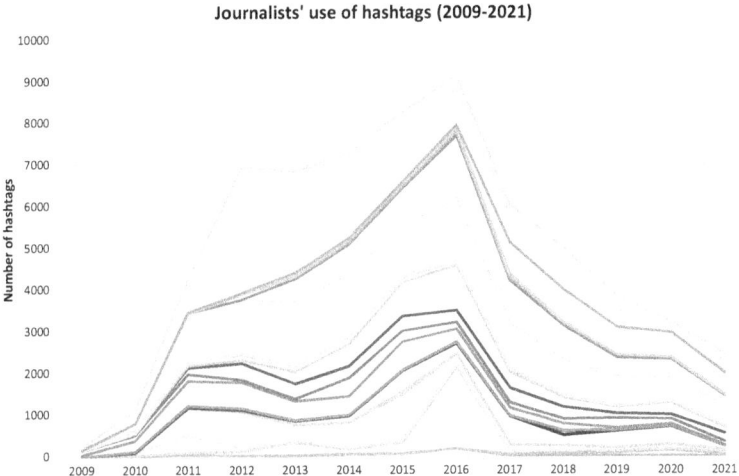

Figure 4.4 Journalists' use of hashtags (2009–2021).

Disruption includes the period of 2009–2011, before the use of hashtags reaches its peak; adaption includes the period of 2012–2016 when the use of hashtags reaches is peak; and normalisation includes the period of 2017–2022, after the use of hashtags reaches its peak, when journalists decide the extent to which they employ this core feature in their tweets (Figure 4.4).

The first peak occurred for most journalists in the period of 2011–2012 and the second one during 2016, after which a steady decline is apparent in all journalists' use of hashtags. That is the use of hashtags for dialogical purposes did not become, through a process of adaption, a part of the news journalist's toolkit and their use was not normalised in any mundane way. In essence the use of hashtags was not regarded as significant for undertaking news journalism and correspondingly their use declines sharply after 2016. Van Dijck (2013, p. 19) frames normalisation as the process that occurs through various adjustments but also 'gradual transformations of the user habits and changing levels of acceptance'. In the case of hashtags, the initial level of acceptance changed over the years, and particularly after 2016.

Journalists used hashtags for dialogical purposes minimally. The majority of journalists opted for using second style of use namely 'official' hashtags – those keywords that were widely accepted by Twitter users in relation to a particular theme. Such 'official' hashtags include for example keywords that are related to elections (e.g., #GE2010;

#GE2015); keywords that are related to certain news topics (such as #PandoraPapers; #Brexit; #EUReferendum; Covid19; #omicron); keywords that are related to live coverage of events (e.g., #PMQs, #leadersdebate); and keywords that are customary for Twitter users (e.g., #ff[8]). Very few journalists use a few humorous hashtags. The use of popular Twitter users' hashtags and particularly the use of customary hashtags that are part of Twitter's culture, such as the #ff one, shows that news journalists simply regarded hashtags as extant features adopted by an organisation or were common parlance by Twitter users. That is hashtags were part of a common 'culture of use' (Burgess & Baym, 2020, p. 21).

The third way that hashtags were used (or not used) was as a form of self-promotion. Specifically, the way participant journalists used the third style of hashtags, that allow them to promote their journalistic work that takes place in another platform or format, such as in broadcasting. For example, in 2014, 80.8% of one journalist's hashtags referred to the news programme she was presenting at the time. This tendency is apparent in many journalists' use of hashtags: 98% of another journalist's hashtags in 2012 concerned a programme he presented and 97% of his hashtags in 2021 referred to a news website he owns; 70% of another journalist's hashtags in 2018 referred to the publication he is the editor of; 82.5% of another jounalist's hashtags in 2021 refer to his work at a broadcast channel; 62% of another journalist's hashtags in 2021 referred to the TV programme she presents. This self-referential use of hashtags demonstrates that they are not used as features of sociality, but rather as enhancements of ones' tweets' visibility, or as promotion of ones' work.

Of the three styles of use through hashtags, the 'official' and the 'promotional' were accommodated and used, because it was convenient, there was no alternative, or it served a self-interested promotional purpose. The first style of use, i.e. using a hashtag for dialogical purposes was not widely employed by the participant journalists. This suggests that whatever coping strategies news journalists adopted, the use of one of Twitter's core affordances was not incorporated in full. This means that it was neither disruptive nor desirable in terms of being adaptively accommodated. The implication is that claims concerning the value of this affordance for news journalism might need to be toned down. The participant news journalists in this study did not adapt their use of Twitter to include enhancing their visibility nor as a means of journalists' inclusion into ongoing conversations on the platform. Indeed, most news journalists who participated in the study used the dialogical style of hashtag use very rarely.

From disruption to normalisation: journalists' Twitter accounts 95

Moving on to Twitter's other core feature, the 'mention', this is considered to be the strongest form of engagement with Twitter and with other users.[9] Burgess and Baym (2020, p. 39) consider this feature as key to

> Twitter's role as a medium for conversation, and essential for creating, maintaining, and enlivening connections among users. In a platform designed 'to announce rather than converse, it is emblematic of users' insistence on their capacity to reorganize in order to socialise.

As with the hashtag, the mention feature was invented by Twitter users in 2009 as means to enhance Twitter's interactive and communicative aspects. Since then, 'the @ has been continuously modified, resisted, and redefined by both users and the company' (Burgess & Baym, 2020, p. 39), but it remains the primary form of discursive exchange among Twitter users. For news journalists, apart from serving communication and networking purposes, this feature allows them to share other actors' work by acknowledging the respective authors or by providing commentary on those actors' original tweets or work (Dagoula, 2017).

All journalists included in the study use this feature, showing adaptive behaviour towards this core affordance, in contrast with the dialogical style of use for hashtags. Some of them use mentions more than others (e.g., journalists Dan Hodges, Marina Hyde, Fraser Nelson, John Rentoul, Popi Tsapanidou and Kostas Vaxevanis), as shown in Figure 4.5.

From an evolutionary point of view (Figure 4.6), the use of mentions by news journalists again presents the same distinct pattern we observed in relation to journalists' activity in the platform and to journalists' use of hashtags. As with the other two indicators, the use of mentions over time reveals a slow start, a peak of activity and a decline.

The stage of disruption includes the period of 2009–2012, before the use of mentions reaches its peak, showing that news journalists recognised Twitter as a tool for interaction with other Twitter users. Regardless of the form of this interaction (e.g., for conversation or for news-gathering purposes), during the disruption stage news journalists engage both with Twitter's 'mention' feature and with other users. Adaptive behaviour (2012–2017) is evidenced again by the stability that follows disruption and is linked to journalists' coping strategies in relation to Twitter's interactive and conversational potential. As Baumgartner and Jones (2009) note, stability can also entail flexibility

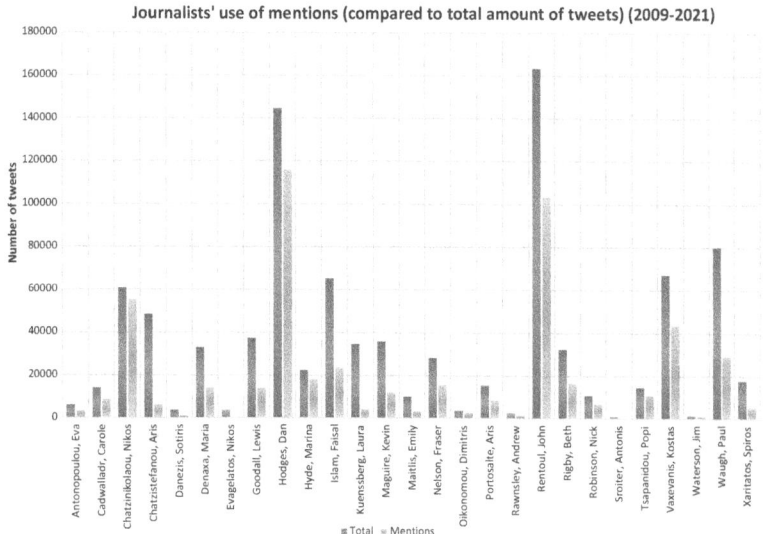

Figure 4.5 Journalists' use of mentions compared to total amount of tweets (2009–2021).

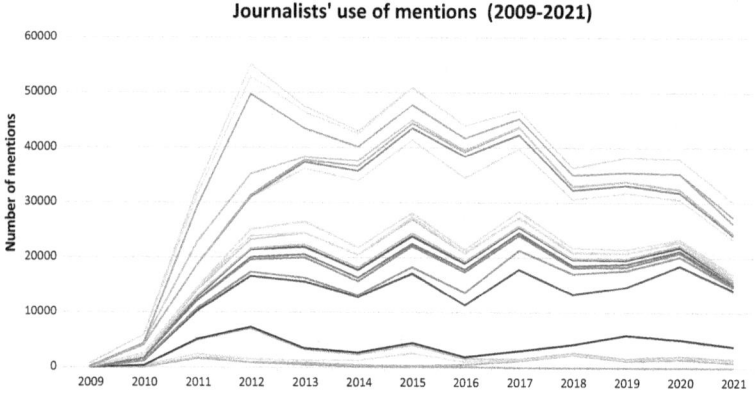

Figure 4.6 Journalists' use of mentions (2009–2021).

that provides the possibility for innovation, and is consequently the stage that journalists decide on whether an innovative approach to their practices (via the use of specific platforms or their constituent features) is appropriate and desirable for them and can be integrated into daily practice. Mid- to long-term normalisation includes the period

From disruption to normalisation: journalists' Twitter accounts 97

of 2017–2021, when news journalists realised the extent to which they employ this core feature in their tweets: for some news journalists it means that they use Twitter primarily as a conversational tool, by continuing to use this feature and to engage with other users extensively. For others, it means that they use Twitter not solely for conversational reasons, but they integrate this feature in their overall use of Twitter, while for others it means that after trying the feature they reject its usefulness for them. Same as the use of hashtags, the first peak occurred for most journalists in the period of 2011–2012 and the second one during 2015, after which a steady decline is apparent in all journalists' use of mentions and replies (and especially after 2020). The normalisation stage (2017–2022) supports Jukes' (2019, p. 255) view that within news journalism there now exists a more relaxed attitude towards social media, and that the 'corporate panic' of early days has faded in the meantime.

Qualitative analysis[10] on the use of mentions demonstrates that most journalists engage with other Twitter users, but also with media and political actors. There are, however, some cases worth-mentioning that use this feature in a different way. For instance, in 2015, 76% of a journalist's tweets that included a mention were self-referential – the journalist mentioned himself, by the use of the linguistic convention 'via @name of journalist, so as to disseminate his journalistic work. 47% of another journalist's tweets in 2021 concerned thank you notes to Twitter users that share his published output. This use of Twitter could be considered as an exemplification of normalisation of the platform, as the studied journalists have chosen to use Twitter's features in a way that aligns with their expected outcomes and desires.

4.4.3 Formatting tweets and textual choices

The third core feature examined in this study concerns the syntax and the textual choices news journalists make on Twitter. This feature, apart from offering an insight into the texture of the news journalists circulate on the platform, allows an understanding of the degree of normalisation of the platform. The analysis of individuals' journalistic accounts reveals that the use of a platform is not univariate, static and inclusive, even though there are commonalities in journalists' syntax, formatting and expressive choices. Their use of Twitter is heterogeneous and this heterogeneity reflects journalists' personalities and is linked with their individual choices regarding Twitter's use. Journalists' textual choices directly reflect different adaptive competencies and coping strategies, as they are defined and unpacked in

Chapter 2. These coping strategies are varieties of short-term adaption utilised to ameliorate or ignore Twitter, or to use Twitter in ways that fit in with each journalist's choices and personality. Equally, journalists' uses of Twitter are the outcome of organisational pressures and contingencies, of changing institutional norms and values, and of the extent to which they have independence from these considerations. During the studied timeframe, coping strategies become attenuated and normalisation occurred.

When it comes to the formatting of tweets, there are no significant variations overall across the studied time period (2009–2021). Within individual journalistic accounts (and for the majority of journalists) the analysis below demonstrates the ways Twitter was normalised and routinised as a work tool. The chosen formatting as well as journalists' textual choices during all years show that news journalists use Twitter primarily to comment on current affairs and to disseminate their work. The 'Headline and Link' format (as well as the mere 'link' one) is the most popular type of formatting of tweets, especially during the short-term disruption stage. This use of Twitter, that resembles an automated feed, shows a less skilful use of Twitter (Engesser & Humprecht, 2015, p. 519) and reveals an experimentation with the platform, by adhering to its minimum requirements. The other types demonstrate further engagement with Twitter, showing evidence of adaption to Twitter's 'cultures of use' and its respective functions. Additionally, the fact that most journalists follow a chosen format in the majority of their tweets alludes to normalisation of the platform. The most common types of tweets encountered in the examined accounts' tweets are presented below.

4.4.3.1 Tweets in the format of: *headline and link*

This is the most standardised type of tweet that includes the title of an article and the link to the source where it was published. This type of tweet includes internal and external to Twitter links, as well as links to journalists' own work or other published journalistic work. Some examples are:

- The case against the 50p tax + link
- March Brexit almost certainly out of reach.... + link

From disruption to normalisation: journalists' Twitter accounts 99

> - We are in Dover tonight for #Newsnight as this tragedy unfolds + link
> - Age of austerity + link

4.4.3.2 Tweets in the format: **commentary + link**

This type of tweet is similar to the previous one; however, in this category, tweets are more personalised, as links are accompanied by journalists' comments that replace neutral headlines. Some examples are:

> - Hadn't clocked that there was a remake of West Side Story directed by Spielberg coming out very soon... + link
> - My bit about the energy crisis (another resilience triumph) + link
> - YEEEEESSSSSSS https://t.co/sURYuOwwLM (Marina Hyde)
> - Good, if long, summary of what is known about super-spreading events & individual variation. + link
> - I'm writing this week's edition of the Guardian tech newsletter, which means if you want to read some exclusive data on what people really watch on Netflix, then you'll have to sign up here to get it. + link

4.4.3.3 Tweets in the format of: **link**

This category was most common during the early years of Twitter (2009, 2010), when some journalists posted only a link without further explanation.

4.4.3.4 Tweets in the format of: **commentary**

The second most common type of tweet after the 'headline + link' one, this category includes tweets which include political comments, journalists' professional opinion, and professionally related commentary. Some examples are:

- As for the predictive power of the data itself...take a look at the confidence intervals.
- When a reshuffle takes this long, with this much briefing about who's getting what job, it's always because someone somewhere has said "no thanks, I'm not doing that" and thrown a spanner in the works.

4.4.3.5 Tweets in the format of: reporting

This category includes tweets that consist of pieces of reporting, usually from a live event. Some examples include:

- Don't know on what, but hearing there will be a statement from Speaker at 3.30- could theoretically be a ruling on whether govt can even hold another meaningful vote.
- PM. We need to slow down the seeding of #omicron.
- Announces stricter testing/isolating regime. 'We are not stopping people travelling but anyone travelling to UK has to take a PCR two days after arrival and isolate until they get a negative result'.

4.4.3.6 Tweets in the format of: personal comments

This category includes tweets with comments that either concern a personal topic or are written in a personal tone and style. Notably, personal tweets are few, showing a rather professional use of the medium by almost all journalists. Some examples are:

- Just landed in #iceland and look what we found! + photo
- I LOVE the BBC Olympics promo
- Sun, flowers and butterflies are out in East Sussex. Glorious day. And petrol stations are open with no queues 😊
- This sounds very dull but I promise you'll thank me for it: Buy a new 20W power adapter to charge your phone. Stop using that one you got with an iPhone in 2014. Your life will, literally, be transformed.

4.4.3.7 Tweets in the format of: personal responses

This category includes tweets that are responses to other Twitter users, but without the use of the feature '@'. An example is:

> • @username[11] I think. Might depend on the quality of candidate Labour puts up against him. (John Rentoul)

Formatting and syntax cannot be separated from journalists' textual choices, which are also heterogeneous. Journalists' textual choices accord to the conventions of Twitter and computer-mediated language, such as the use of non-standard orthography, the abridged posts (Zappavigna, 2013, pp. 19–22) and the use of affective language (Papacharissi, 2014). Barton and Lee (2013, p. 5) discuss a 'new variety' of language, that appears in the computer-mediated communication characterised by a series of elements, such as: Acronyms and initialisms (e.g., lol for laughing out loud); word reductions (e.g., gd for good); letter/number homophones (e.g., U for 'you' or 2 for 'to'); stylised spelling (e.g., 'I am sooooooooooo happy'); emoticons (e.g., :) for smiling, :(for being sad) and unconventional/stylised punctuation (e.g., '!!!!!!!!'). This 'new variety' of language is apparent in the tweets of the examined news journalists' accounts over the whole period 2009–2021. This use of language, that differs from the tone and formality of their reporting, shows adaption and subsequent normalisation of their practices to Twitter's conventions. First, by following the 'concision requirement' and second, by adjusting (to some extent) to the platform's linguistic conventions

Studying linguistic mannerisms, styles of expression and vocabulary is crucial if for no other reason than linguistic conventions on Twitter are constantly changing (Page et al., 2014, pp. 27–30) and accordingly are 'highly temporally bound'. From an evolutionary point of view, it is possible to discern evolutionary stages according to how and when these conventions change. And this can only be done via analysis of the formatting and textual choices used in each individual's account. Below are three of the most characteristic examples that demonstrate an evolutionary move from disruption to normalisation via the use of Twitter in terms of format and textual choices.

For example, for one journalist we observe that in 2010, when she started using Twitter, she was posting primarily comments, both professional and personal. In 2011, when her account presented the highest activity, she used Twitter mainly to communicate with Twitter users: 80% of her tweets are replies to other users. In 2020 and 2021 her account presents minimal activity and her tweets are a mix of responses to other users, commentary on current affairs, and dissemination of links that aim to promote either her work or her employers. Linguistically, there is also an apparent difference. In the first years of Twitter, her tweets were informal and written in a hybrid language blend called 'greeklish'.[12] In her recent posts, the journalist uses a more formal tone, and her tweets are mainly written in Greek.

Another journalist, began to use Twitter in 2010; his account included commentary, replies to other users (62%), invitations to users to follow his journalistic work in other media platforms (e.g., broadcasting), and tweets in the format of 'headline + link' through which he promoted his journalistic output, as the links lead directly to his publication page (external website). In 2021, when he used Twitter the most, his account is dedicated to thank Twitter users for sharing his work. His tweets are presented in two formats: either as direct replies to Twitter users (50% of the tweets), or as thank you notes to users, as shown by the example:

- Thank you, *name of Twitter user.* + link to Twitter user's original tweet that usually includes a link to the journalist's publication

For another journalist, in 2009, when he started using Twitter, his account included only tweets in the format 'headline + link'. His account was connected to his personal blog hosted in his employer's website and resembled an automated feed. In 2017, when he used Twitter the most, we observe a shift towards commentary, provision of internal and external links, and responses to other Twitter users, a practice that he continued to follow also in 2021.

While these examples clearly depict changes in specific journalistic accounts from 2009 to 2021, changes are apparent in all of the other accounts to varying degrees. These changes concern the formatting of the tweets, the tonality, the textual and the linguistic choices journalists make (e.g., grammar, or inclusion of emojis). In some cases, changes are distinct – for instance, in 2011, one journalist used Twitter in his personal capacity; however, he now uses it exclusively in his professional capacity and mostly to promote the show he is presenting on television. In other cases, changes are less pronounced. In other words, these transformations in journalists' behaviour and respectively the changing levels of acceptance and adaption show that the change that occurred in their use of Twitter is of an evolutionary nature. For example, one journalist's tweets consisted mostly of commentary and links since 2010 (when he first started using Twitter); however, the tonality has changed as well as the type of links he shares – in 2021, he mostly shares links to journalistic output published in his employer's website.

The formatting of tweets and textual choices reveals that style and language matter within and in terms of the constraints imposed by Twitter's technical configuration. In that sense, it is a fixed environment with mechanical boundaries that cannot be crossed. Unless the platform is reengineered Twitter is nothing other than a set of limited possibilities. It is the extent to which those possibilities are used and the causes they serve that is important to understand. In the case of the participating journalists, they stayed within the traditional conventions of news journalism. New choices on presentation did not mean radical departure toward abandoning professionally acceptable standards of behaviour. Not everything is capable of adaptation. Some things need to be adapted to while others, because of new exigencies, need to be abandoned. Regarding news journalism they mastered Twitter through constant adaption and normalisation which led to moderate changes. Where Twitter threatens to undermine certain forms of news journalism is discussed in the next chapter in terms of threats to our contemporary civil information order.

Notes

1 All news journalists selected for the study have public accounts on Twitter. On that basis, and considering the high number of their followers on the platform, news journalists in this study are considered as public figures acting in their public capacity.

In addition, and according to Twitter's regulation, information used in this study do not contain any sensitive information as this is defined by Twitter and fully adhere to Twitter's definition of 'public data' (Twitter, 2022).
2 This criterion is adjusted to the language limitation. Given that all Greek journalists post their tweets in Greek, their respective numbers of followers are lower than the U.K. journalists.
3 In some cases, the table includes more than one tweets, so as to better highlight the discussed awkwardness.
4 Information provided here accessed 25 April 2022.
5 Twitter allows users to present themselves in no more than 160 characters. This concision requirement is different to the one that concerns the tweets, as these can be up to 280 characters.
6 For the distinction of the patterns, the majority of journalists' accounts was taken into account.

7 According to Van Dijck et al. (2018: 53), datafication is prescribed in platforms as a key mechanism and suggests that every form of user interaction can be captured as data (e.g., user metrics).
8 #FF is the abbreviation of the hashtag #FollowFriday which Twitter users use to highlight their favorite Twitter accounts, by recommending to their followers' accounts that they consider worth-following on Twitter. The #FF Twitter tradition started in 2009.
9 The study includes information about two core features: hashtags and mentions. However, the latter also includes retweets and quote tweets. Methodologically and analytically, both retweets and quote tweets are considered as means of interaction with specific users. Here, mentions and quote tweets are examined under the 'mentions' category, whilst retweets are excluded.
10 Qualitative analysis was conducted for each journalist for three distinct years: the year they started using Twitter, the year they used mentions the most, and the last year included in the examined time period (2021).
11 User Twitter handles are anonymised.
12 Greeklish is a blend of Greek and English language. It is an informal type of writing where the Greek language is written using the Latin alphabet. The use of this hybrid linguistic format is used primarily in computer-mediated communication, and it was very popular during the early 2000s.

5 An evaluation of the direct and indirect costs and benefits of Twitter to news journalism

The civil and political influence of Twitter exceeds the number of users it has if for no other reason than Twitter is used by so many news journalists. It is both a tool for news journalists and a source for news journalism. That said, it is most definitely not an agora, town square, public assembly, virtual town hall, a facilitator of deliberative public discourse or the consciousness of the world. As a tool for news, journalists use Twitter to suit their own purposes, while as a source of news it is a mixture of the toxic, the relevant and the insightful (Burgess, 2022). In essence, it is both valued and reviled,[1] and it is full of yet to be realised potential. It is the penetration of news journalism by Twitter that makes it of interest and the fact that it has become a platform of choice for politicians, parties and supporters. Why should such a tool be so pervasive in news journalism? Perhaps because of the blindingly obvious – it is so convenient and easy to use as well as being extensively used by politicians, parties and their supporters. It is also built for scaling up and as a vehicle for generating revenues. It is hard to escape the fact that this is true albeit a truism. And that not much else about Twitter in terms of the many promises that surrounded it are true. But if this is so, what does it signify for news journalism?

In Chapter 1, the dominant theories of Twitter's impact on news journalism were reviewed, and I argued that it should be examined and considered through the evolutionary theory known as punctuated equilibrium. I further argued that this theory would shed light on what Twitter changed or confirmed about the practices and values of news journalism, and what benefits and costs accrued with its widespread acceptance within news organisations. Via a longitudinal study, I wished to establish whether Twitter has disrupted the institution of news journalism to produce new practices and forms of news journalism, but also whether it has altered the core of news journalism practice. Conveniently, punctuated equilibrium breaks down into three phases of change that have different outcomes and can readily be empirically identified: disruption is frequently likened to 'smashing things to see what survives' but in fact, as noted in Chapter 2, disruption is both a displacement event and a commonplace event. As for the velocity of change, it could be measured through the rate in which news journalism (news organisations and news journalists) adapted to Twitter. This second stage can be likened to an experimental stage – where Twitter was appropriated by news journalism as the tool for their own discrete needs. Studies revealed all the various attitudes journalists and organisations had towards Twitter. But ultimately, adaption assumes the form of the self-interest of the news organisation and the habits of individual reporters with very little else being of concern. Ideals regarding new audiences, participatory sourcing and co-production of news and new types of journalism were subject to news organisations' obsessive calculation: could these practices be leveraged towards helping news journalism find a sustainable future (evolutionary survival)? Accordingly, new journalistic practices were tried and in part accepted or rejected entirely; the outcomes being the normalisation of Twitter – as a tool and a source. This third stage consisted of the acceptance of those adaptive practices deemed by news organisations to retain core values, facilitate practical matters of news gathering and reporting and to anticipate the needs of audiences thereby contributing to the sustainability of the news organisation. In other words, this evolutionary process of punctuated equilibrium provides for a three-stage account of sustainability qua survival through adaption.

But the question of why Twitter should be so pervasive in news journalism remains. Punctuated equilibrium helps us to answer that question. If the idea of Twitter was that it would benefit news journalism, it did so because it stood for nothing less than the 'retooling' of news journalism. But 'retooling' has both a material element and a depth element. The former was discussed by academics (in Chapter 2) and news journalists (in Chapter 3) in terms of how Twitter had changed news journalism itself. The latter entails understanding what these changes signify (if anything) for, in our case, practicing journalists (in Chapter 4). The study undertaken was guided by these two accounts of Twitter's impact and enables us to conclude with an overall evaluation of the benefits and costs to the practice of news journalism. What follows is first a summary of the benefits and costs and then an assessment of their actual significance for the practice of news journalism.

Costs and benefits of Twitter to news journalism 107

To summarise: the benefits to the practice of news journalism were said to consist of Twitter as an immersive all-encompassing news background – the new news vibe. Gone was the traditional structured and deterministic news cycle, in its place 'ambient' news provided instantaneity and immediacy within which news journalists were the pre-eminent sense makers. A further benefit, related to this, was that Twitter was the embodiment of a global village. On offer here was global reach, public intimacy and improved journalism driven by always-on communication technologies, that included contributions by a wide variety of users. The networked and engaged audience for news journalism had arrived offering a greater source of news as well as a greater audience for news. In short, Twitter was the new 'newswire.'

Looking at the benefits through a slightly different prism, tweets represented the new *vox populi*, or more prosaically, revealed what public sentiment and opinion were concerned with. The proximal journalist was, it was argued, closer to their public than ever before. The news journalist now had to consider how they should represent themselves to their audience(s). This was not just a case of marketing 'one's own digital self' via a 'digital business card' or even branding one's digital self but also of 'engaging in conversation' and displaying trustworthiness. There was even a negative benefit in this – a journalist could respond more rapidly to misunderstandings about what they did or did not report and or respond to information disorders surrounding news events. The final benefit touted was that news journalists now enjoyed a closer relationship with their traditional elite sources and consequently could glean a greater understanding of events alongside which – they could also guarantee anonymity (to whistle-blowers) since Twitter allows users to operate pseudonymously.

The costs to the practice of news journalism were perceived to be that with instantaneity and immediacy came increased professional pressure that affected both the quality of news reporting and the extent to which reports were based on thorough investigation and were therefore accurate. Compounding this situation was that news organisations equated competitiveness with speed of response to Twitter led stories, while journalists saw the threat to their competitiveness in terms of missing out on pieces of information. This latter point was emphasised by the fact that news organisations now had at their disposal an abundance of metrics and datafication processes which could inform news organisation managers about a particular journalist's popularity, readership, attractiveness to advertisers and ultimately their employability. Other costs (for some) included that the news journalist's reliance on elite sources increased and engagement with audiences did not materialise.

However, these costs were not perceived to be the most harmful to news journalism. Far from it. Twitter had itself evolved into a 'toxic place' (Amnesty International, 2018). Here free speech justifications, the lack of content moderation and a libertarian sensibility combine to permit extremist and partisan agendas and attacks. It is the increasing sophistication of these attacks and agendas that poses the biggest threat to the quality and accuracy of news journalism. Alongside this, such toxicity also encourages the targeting of news journalists (especially female news journalists) with recent evidence suggesting that such targeting increases the pressure on journalists to self-censor (Harrison & Pukallus 2018, Pukallus et al., 2020) and, as recently reported (Posetti et al., 2020), targeting can and does precede physical attacks. The sum of this charge of toxicity is that Twitter is an essential tool in processes of information disorder and antagonism which has brought about (in part) the coarsening of political discourse into slogans and inaugurated further processes of 'diffused toxicity'.

The question now is not how coherent these charges are – as Chapters 1–3 have shown they all exist against a background of analytical coherence and empirical detail – but what their significance might be for the practice of news journalism. Do they accurately describe the opportunities and constraints on journalists doing their job? And is the truism – that Twitter is so convenient and easy to use as well as being extensively used by politicians, parties and their supporters, it is also built for scaling up and as a vehicle for generating revenues – correct?

From the interviews described in Chapter 4, news journalists (or at least the cohort I interviewed) argued that the core values of news journalism – accuracy, sincerity and objectivity to report the news truthfully (Harrison, 2019b) – had not changed. Nor was Twitter perceived to have shattered the norms and mores of institutionalised news journalism. News organisations did not reconceive of themselves as Twitter enabled nor did Twitter require them to differentiate between new and old types of news journalism. The proximity of news journalists to audience accommodated in terms of style and rhetoric rather than content. In essence:

> the civil ideal of the news remains as a promise of the news's contribution to civil life and liberal democratic culture and, as such, is an important part of both journalists' and audiences' imaginaries. The plain fact is that the civil ideal of news and the grounded

reality of news coexist and constantly engage each other in different ways, in different conditions and under diverse circumstances both positively and negatively.

(Harrison, 2019, p. 65)

Then and now there remains in news journalists a systemic distrust of dramatic and sensational claims and unsubstantiated assertions. Interestingly at the end of every interview conducted in this study the participating news journalists were asked whether their final evaluation of Twitter was positive or negative in terms of its benefits and costs. With some varying degrees of hesitancy, all replied that overall, the scale leans towards the benefits. Certainly, Twitter has facilitated changes in newsroom practices, news gathering and news cycles as well as the look and feel of news have all been influenced by the nature of Twitter, but their significances are contextualised by journalists' comments to the effect that newsrooms have always evolved responding to perceived crises. In short, changes in newsrooms constantly occur in a progressive evolutionary way not a revolutionary way. In this light disruption is seen as both inevitable – if we assume that communication technologies offer different tools for news journalists to use – and that it will follow the same pattern of evolutionary punctuated equilibrium.

Presently the issue of toxicity and how to deal with it, represents the current disruptive event regarding the institution of news journalism and its engagement with advances in communication technologies and the associated civil and political issues that derive from these advances. Free speech absolutists and first amendment fanatics, vie with those who wish to restrain hate speech, group libel and exclusionary politics through the perennial debate as to how to balance free speech with regulation.[2] Inevitably news organisations are becoming implicated in terms of how they see the future of media regulation as it affects them. To be clear Twitter is just a small part an information ecosystem that many believe needs to be constrained. It is not a singularly special force that accounts for all things toxic, nor is it even the most egregious case of the toxic poisoning of forbearance. Rather, Twitter is part of a broader platform ecosystem that is subject to evolutionary change according to the patter of disruption, adaption, and normalisation. To repeat the point made in Chapter 2:

> Because social change is endemic in modern societies, it is hardly surprising that the history of journalism has been marked by continuous eruptions of crisis. Just as current anxieties have been triggered by computerization and digital news, so were earlier

crises of journalism linked to technological shifts that demanded new forms of economic organization.

(Alexander, 2016, p. 3)

Here crises represent a series of punctuation disruptive events, with the latest toxicity creating the conditions for demands for new forms of media regulation.

Notes

1. John Naughton (2022) recently wrote that Twitter is 'one small private shop (...) in which hyperventilating elites, trolls, journalists and millions of bots hang out and fight with one another'.
2. Two things affecting the issues of regulation have occurred simultaneously in 2022. First: the EU's Digital Services Act (DSA) has recently received provisional support from the European Council and European Parliament (2022). The stated aim of the DSA is to make the Internet a safer space for European citizens. To this end it has adopted the maxim that 'what is illegal offline must be illegal online' to this end it covers matters of Governance, Online marketplaces, Systemic risks of very large platforms and search engines, Dark patterns Recommender systems, Crisis mechanism and Protecting minors online. Second Elon Musk under the banner of free speech absolutism is trying to buy Twitter. Whether he succeeds or not the clear statement made by Musk is that Twitter must do more to (a) promote free speech and (b) react to attempts to constrain free speech. Unifying these two things Naughton (Observer 2022) noted that Thierry Breton, the EU's commissioner for the internal market, warned that Twitter must follow European rules on moderating illegal and harmful content online, even after it goes private: 'We welcome everyone,' said Breton. 'We are open but, on our conditions... 'Elon, there are rules. You are welcome but these are our rules. It's not your rules which will apply here'".

References

Alexander, J.C. (2020). The Cultural Sociology of Political Performance, Icons, and Social Media, with Prof. Jeffrey Alexander [Audio podcast episode]. In *Social Media and Politics*. M. Bossetta, https://socialmediaandpolitics.org/cultural-sociology-political-performance-social-media-politics-jeffrey-alexander/.

Alexander, J.C. (2016). Introduction, In J.C. Alexander, E. Butler Breese & M. Luengo (Eds.) *The Crisis of Journalism Reconsidered: Democratic Culture, Professional Codes, Digital Future* (pp. 1-28). Cambridge University Press.

Alexander, J.C., Butler Breese, E., & Luengo, M. (2016). *The Crisis of Journalism Reconsidered: Democratic Culture, Professional Codes, Digital Future.* Cambridge University Press.

Alexander, J.C., Thompson, K., & Desfor Edles, L. (2008). *A Contemporary Introduction to Sociology: Culture and Society in Transition* (2nd ed.). Routledge.

Amnesty International. (2018). Toxic Twitter: A toxic place for women. https://bit.ly/3yLT6GL.

Aral, S. (2021). *The Hype Machine: How Social Media Disrupts Our Elections, Our Economy, and Our Health - and How We Must Adapt.* Currency.

Armstrong, C.L., & Gao, F. (2010). Now Tweet This: How News Organizations Use Twitter. *Electronic News*, 4(4), 218–235.

Arthur, C. (2009, August 6). Read It and Weep: Evan Williams of Twitter on Newsnight - The Transcript. *The Guardian.* https://bit.ly/384nVvm.

Artwick, C.G. (2013). Reporters on Twitter. *Digital Journalism*, 1(2), 212–228.

Bail, C. (2021). *Breaking the Social Media Prism: How to Make Our Platforms Less Polarizing.* Princeton University Press.

Barnard, S. (2016). Tweet or Be Sacked: Twitter and the New Elements of Journalistic Practice. *Journalism*, 17(2), 190–207.

Barnidge, M., Heath, W., Zhang J., & Broussard, R. (2020). Business as Usual? A Social Capital Approach to Understanding Interactions with Journalists on Twitter. *Journalism Studies*, 21(3), 406–424.

References

Barthel, M. L., Moon, R., & Mari, W. (2015, March 05). Who Retweets Whom: How Digital and Legacy Journalists Interact on Twitter? *Tow Center for Digital Journalism*. https://bit.ly/3FZJObA.
Barton, D., & Lee, C. (2013). *Language Online: Investigating Digital Texts and Practices*. Routledge.
Baumgartner, F.R., & Jones, B.D. (2009). *Agendas and Instability in American Politics*. The University of Chicago Press.
Bech Sillesen, L. (2015, March-April). Analyzing Journalists' Twitter Bios. *Columbia Journalism Review*. https://www.cjr.org/analysis/analyzing_journalists_twitter_bios.php.
Bell, E., & Owen, T. (2017). The Platform Press: How Silicon Valley Reengineered Journalism. *Tow Center for Digital Journalism*. https://bit.ly/380bsIZ.
Benton, J. (2014, May 15). The Leaked New York Times Innovation Report Is One of the Key Documents of This Media Age. *NiemanLab*. https://bit.ly/3lqj8rh.
Boczkowski, P. (2004). *Digitizing the News*. The MIT Press.
Bossio, D., & Nelson, J.L. (2021). Reconsidering Innovation: Situating and Evaluating Change in Journalism. *Journalism Studies*, 22(11), 1377–1381.
Bouvier, G., & Rosenbaum, J. E. (2020). *Twitter, the Public Sphere, and the Chaos of Online Deliberation*. Palgrave Macmillan.
Brems, C., Temmerman, M., Graham, T., & Broersma, M. (2016), Personal Branding on Twitter. *Digital Journalism*, 5(4), 443–459.
Broersma, M., & Graham, T. (2012). Social Media as Beat: Tweets as a News Source during the 2010 British and Dutch Elections. *Journalism Practice*, 6(3), 403–419.
Broersma, M., & Graham, T. (2016). Tipping the Balance of Power: Social Media and the Transformation of Political Journalism, In A. Bruns, G. Enli, E. Skogerbø, A.O. Larsson & C. Christensen (Eds.), *The Routledge Companion to Social Media and Politics* (pp. 89–103). Routledge.
Bruno, N. (2011). Tweet First, Verify Later? How Real-Time Information Is Changing the Coverage of Worldwide Crisis Events. *Oxford: Reuters Institute for the Study of Journalism*. https://bit.ly/3wwUOce.
Bruns, A. (2005). *Gatewatching: Collaborative Online News Production*. Peter Lang.
Bruns, A. (2018). *Gatewatching and News Curation: Journalism, Social Media, and the Public Sphere*. Peter Lang Publishing.
Bruns, A. (2021). Gatewatching and News Curation. In J. Morrison, J. Birks, & M. Berry (Eds.), *The Routledge Companion to Political Journalism* (pp. 252–261). Routledge.
Burgess, J. (2022, April 27). The 'Digital Town Square'? What Does It Mean When Billionaires Own the Online Spaces Where We Gather?. *The Conversation*. https://bit.ly/3yOfKhz.
Burgess, J., & Baym, N. (2020). *Twitter: A Biography*. NYU Press.
Calore, M. (2007, March 9). Twitter is Ruling SXSW. *Wired*. https://www-wired-com.proxy-ub.rug.nl/2007/03/twitter-is-ruling-sxsw/.
Canter, L. (2014). Personalised Tweeting. *Digital Journalism*, 3(6), 888–907.

References

Chadha, K., & Wells, R. (2016). Journalistic Responses to Technological Innovation in Newsrooms. *Digital Journalism*, 4(8), 1020–1035.

Chadwick, A. (2013). *The Hybrid Media System*. Oxford University Press.

Chadwick, A. (2017). *The Hybrid Media System* (2nd ed.). Oxford University Press.

Cowls, J., & Schroeder, R. (2018). Tweeting All the Way to the White House. In P.J. Boczkowski & Z. Papacharissi (Eds.), *Trump and the Media* (pp. 151–157). MIT Press.

Curran, J., Fenton, N., & Freedman, D. (2016). *Misunderstanding the Internet* (2nd ed.). Routledge.

Dagoula, C. (2012). *Journalism in the Social Media Era* [Unpublished master's thesis]. Aristotle University of Thessaloniki. https://bit.ly/38vBrIN.

Dagoula, C. (2017). *The Ongoing Structural Transformations of the Digital Public Sphere(s): The Role of Journalism* [Doctoral dissertation, The University of Sheffield]. White Rose eTheses Online. http://etheses.whiterose.ac.uk/18499/.

Dagoula, C. (2019). *Mapping the Greek Journalistic Twitter: A Theoretical and Empirical Approach*. Metamesonykties.

Dayter, D. (2016). *Discursive Self in Microblogging: Speech Acts, Stories and Self-praise*. John Benjamins Publishing Company.

Deuze, M. (1999). Journalism and The Web. *Gazette*, 61(5), 373–390.

Dubois, E., & Blank, G. (2018). The Echo Chamber Is Overstated: The Moderating Effect of Political Interest and Diverse Media. *Information, Communication & Society*, 21(5), 729–745.

Ebner, M., & Schiefner, M. (2008). Microblogging - More Than Fun?. In A. Sánchez, & P.I. Isaías (Eds.), *IADIS Mobile Learning Conference* (pp. 155–159). Algarve.

Eldredge, N., & Gould, S.J. (1972). Punctuated Equilibria: An Alternative to Phyletic Gradualism. In T.J. Schopf (Ed.), *Models in Paleobiology* (pp. 305–322). Freeman, Cooper & Co.

Engesser, S., & Humprecht, E. (2015) Frequency or Skillfulness: How professional news media use Twitter in five Western countries. *Journalism Studies*, 16(4), 513–529.

Farhi, P. (2009). The Twitter Explosion. *American Journalism Review*, 31(3) https://bit.ly/3RBGs2Q

Fenton, N. (2016). The Internet of me (and my 'friends'). In J. Curran, N. Fenton, & D. Freedman (Eds.), *Misunderstanding the Internet* (2nd ed.) (pp. 145–172). Routledge.

Franklin, B., & Canter, L. (2019). *Digital Journalism Studies: The Key Concepts* (1st ed.). Routledge.

Fuchs, C. (2013). *Social Media: A Critical Introduction*. SAGE Publications.

García de Torres, E., Rost, Al., Calderín, M. et al. (2011, April 1–4). *See You on Facebook or Twitter? The Use of Social Media By 27 News Outlets From 9 Regions in Argentina, Colombia, Mexico, Peru, Portugal, Spain and Venezuela* [Paper presentation]. 12th International Symposium on Online Journalism, Austin, Texas, USA.

Gillespie, T. (2018). *Custodians of the Internet: Platforms, Content Moderation, and the Hidden Decisions that Shape Social Media*. Yale University Press.

Givel, M. (2010). The Evolution of the Theoretical Foundations of Punctuated Equilibrium Theory in Public Policy. *Review of Policy Research*, 27(2), 187–198.

Gould, S.J. (1982). The Meaning of Punctuated Equilibrium and its Role in Validating a Hierarchical Approach to Macroevolution. *Scientia*, 77(18), 135.

Grossman, L. (2009, June 17). Iran's Protests : Why Twitter Is the Medium of the Movement. *Time*. https://bit.ly/3sGynAc

Gulyas, A. (2013). The Influence of Professional Variables on Journalists' Uses and Views of Social Media. *Digital Journalism*, 1(2), 270–285.

Gulyas, A. (2016). Social Media and Journalism. In B. Franklin & S. Eldridge (Eds.), *The Routledge Companion to Digital Journalism Studies* (pp. 396–406). Routledge.

Hanusch F., & Bruns, A. (2017). Journalistic Branding on Twitter: A Representative Study of Australian Journalists' Profile Descriptions. *Digital Journalism*, 5(1), 26–43.

Harrison, J. (2019a). *The Civil Power of the News*. Palgrave Macmillan.

Harrison, J. (2019b). Public Service Journalism. *Oxford Research Encyclopaedia of Communication*. https://bit.ly/3sOzAFy

Harrison, J., & Pukallus, S. (2022). The Civil Norm Building Role of News Journalism in Post-civil War Settings. *Journalism*, 1–19.

Harrison, J., & Pukallus, S. (2018). The Politics of Impunity: A Study of Journalists' Experiential Accounts of Impunity in Bulgaria, Democratic Republic of Congo, India, Mexico and Pakistan. *Journalism*, 22(2), 303–319.

Hassel, A. (2020). Shared Emotion: The Social Amplification of Partisan News on Twitter. *Digital Journalism*, 9(8), 1085–1102.

Hedman, U. (2016). When Journalists Tweet: Disclosure, Participatory and Personal Transparency. *Social Media + Society*, 2(1), 1–13.

Hedman, U. (2020). Making the Most of Twitter: How Technological Affordances Influence Swedish Journalists' Self-branding. *Journalism*, 21(5), 670–687.

Hedman, U. & Djerf-Pierre, M. (2013). The Social Journalist. *Digital Journalism*, 1(3), 368–385.

Hermida, A. (2010). Twittering the News. *Journalism Practice*, 4(3), 297–308.

Hermida, A. (2012). Social Journalism: Exploring How Social Media Is Shaping Journalism. In E. Siapera & A. Veglis (Eds.), *The Handbook of Global Online Journalism (Handbooks in Communication and Media)* (pp. 309–328). Wiley & Blackwell.

Hermida, A. (2013). #Journalism. *Digital Journalism*, 1(3), 295–313.

Hermida, A. (2014). Twitter as an Ambient News Network. In K. Weller, A. Bruns, J. Burgess, M. Mahrt, & C. Puschmann (Eds.), *Twitter and Society* (pp. 359–372). Peter Lang.

Hermida, A. (2016). Social Media and the News. In T. Witschge, C.W. Anderson, D. Domingo, & A. Hermida (Eds.), *The SAGE Handbook of Digital Journalism* (pp. 81–94). SAGE publications.

Higgins, M. (2017, October 24). Mediated Populism, Culture and Media Form. *Nature (Palgrave Communications)*. https://bit.ly/3yNgpQk.

Highfield, T. (2016). *Social Media and Everyday Politics*. Polity Press.

Honeycutt, C., & Herring, S. (2009, January 5–8). *Beyond Microblogging: Conversation and Collaboration via Twitter* [Paper presentation]. 42nd Hawaii International Conference on System Sciences, Waikoloa, HI, USA. https://bit.ly/3sKcQH3.

Howard, P.N. (2020). *Lie Machines: How to Save Democracy from Troll Armies, Deceitful Robots, Junk News Operations, and Political Operatives*. Yale University Press.

Huberman, B.A., Romero, D.M., & Wu, F. (2008). Social Networks That Matter: Twiter Under the Microscope. *First Monday*, 14(1), 1–9. https://bit.ly/3NrVG94.

Jardin, X. (2004, August 11). We Are All Journalists Now. *Wired*. https://bit.ly/3yO0UaR.

Jarvis, J. (2019, January 27). Journalism Is the Conversation. The Conversation Is Journalism. *Medium*. https://bit.ly/3lpeolp.

Java, A., Finin, T., Song, X., & Tseng, B. (2007, August). *Why We Twitter: Understanding Microblogging Usage and Communities* [Paper presentation]. WebKDD and 1st SNA-KDD 2007 workshop on Web mining and social network analysis, California, USA.

Johnson, K.A. (2020). I Got a New Puppy! The Impact of Personal, Opinion, and Objective Tweets on a Journalist's and a News Organization's Perceived Credibility. *Journalism Practice*, 14(1), 48–66.

Johnson, M., Paulussen S., & van Aeist, P. (2018). Much Ado About Nothing? The Low Importance of Twitter as a Sourcing Tool for Economic Journalists. *Digital Journalism*, 6(7), 869–888.

Johnson, S. (2009, June 5). 'How Twitter Will Change the Way We Live. *Time*. https://bit.ly/3G1HjFF.

Jukes, S. (2019). Crossing the Line between News and the Business of News: Exploring Journalists' Use of Twitter. *Media and Communication*, 7(1), 248–258.

Jungherr, A., Rivero, G., & Gayo-Avello, D. (2020). *Retooling Politics: How Digital Media Are Shaping Democracy*. Cambridge University Press.

Kale, S. (2021, December 27). Social Media Is a Bad Feelings Machine. Why Can't We Just Turn It Off for Good? *The Guardian*. https://bit.ly/3LvipPV.

Kreiss, D. (2016). 3- Beyond Administrative Journalism: Civic Skepticism and the Crisis in Journalism. In J.C. Alexander, E. Butler Breese, E., & M Luengo (Eds.), *The Crisis of Journalism Reconsidered: Democratic Culture, Professional Codes, Digital Future* (pp. 59–76). Cambridge University Press.

Lasorsa, D.L., Lewis, S.C., & Holton, A.E. (2012). Normalizing Twitter: Journalism Practice in an Emerging Communication Space. *Journalism Studies*, 13(1), 19–36.

Lawrence, R.G. (2015). Campaign News in the Time of Twitter. In V.A. Farrar-Myers & J.S. Vaughn (Eds.), *Controlling the Message: New Media in American Political Campaigns* (pp. 93–112). New York University Press.

Lee Hughes, A., & Palen, L. (2009, May). *Twitter Adoption and Use in Crisis* [Paper presentation]. Proceedings of the 6th International ISCRAM Conference. Gothenburg, Sweden.

Lee, J. (2015). The Double-Edged Sword: The Effects of Journalists' Social Media Activities on Audience Perceptions of Journalists and Their News Products. *Journal of Computer-Mediated Communication*, 20(3), 312–329.

Lee, J. (2020). "Friending" Journalists on Social Media: Effects on Perceived Objectivity and Intention to Consume News. *Journalism Studies*, 21(15), 2096–2112.

Lewis, S.C., Zamith, R., & Coddington, M. (2020). Online Harassment and Its Implications for the Journalist–Audience Relationship. *Digital Journalism*, 8(8), 1047–1067.

Lieberman, M. (2020, July 28). A Growing Group of Journalists Has Cut Back on Twitter, or Abandoned It Entirely. *Poynter*. https://bit.ly/3sIr7E8.

Lothian-McLean, M. (2022, April, 3). Twitter Is Strictly for the Birds: Never Am I More Disconnected Than When Plugged In. *The Guardian*. https://bit.ly/3lpdXaK.

Luengo, M., & Herrera-Damas, S. (Eds.) (2021). *News Media Innovation Reconsidered: Ethics and Values in a Creative Reconstruction of Journalism*. Wiley-Blackwell.

Maares, P., Lind, F., & Greussing, E. (2020). Showing off Your Social Capital: Homophily of Professional Reputation and Gender in Journalistic Networks on Twitter. *Digital Journalism*, 9(4), 500–517.

Madianou, M., & Miller, D. (2011). *Migration and New Media: Transnational Families and Polymedia*. Routledge.

Manucci, L. (2017). Populism and the Media. In C.R. Kaltwasser, P. Taggart, P. Ochoa Espejo, & P. Ostiguy (Eds.), *The Oxford Handbook of Populism*. Oxford Handbooks Online. https://bit.ly/3Nt7h7N.

Marwick, A.E., & boyd, d., (2010). I Tweet Honestly, I Tweet Passionately: Twitter Users, Context Collapse, and the Imagined Audience. *New Media & Society*, 13(1), 114–133.

Mayfield, A. (2008). *What Is Social Media?* iCrossing. https://bit.ly/3PoShcR

McGonagle, T. (2017). "Fake news": False Fears or Real Concerns? *Netherlands Quarterly of Human Rights*, 35(4), 203–209.

McGregor, S., & Molyneux, L. (2020). Twitter's Influence on News Judgment: An Experiment Among Journalists. *Journalism*, 21(5), 597–613.

McLuhan, M. (1962). *The Gutenberg Galaxy: The Making of Typographic Man*. University of Toronto Press.

Mellado, C., & Alfaro A. (2020). Platforms, Journalists, and Their Digital Selves. *Digital Journalism*, 8(10), 1258–1279.

Mellado, C., & Hermida, A. (2021). A Conceptual Framework for Journalistic Identity on Social Media: How the Personal and Professional Contribute to Power and Profit. *Digital Journalism*, 10(2), 284–299.

Messner, M., Linke, M.S., & Eford, As. (2011). *Shoveling Tweets: An Analysis of the Microblogging Engagement of Traditional News Organizations*

[Paper presentation]. In International Symposium on Online Journalism, UT Austin.
Miller, C. (2011, May 11) #bbcsms: Changing Journalists' Social Media Mindset. *BBC College of Journalism Blog*. https://bbc.in/3t8P7Az.
Mills, A., Chen, R., Lee, J., & Rao, H.R. (2007). Web 2.0 Emergency Applications: How Useful Can Twitter Be for Emergency Response. *Journal of Information Privacy and Security*, 5(3), 3–26.
Min, S.J., & Fink, K. (2021). Keeping Up with the Technologies: Distressed Journalistic Labor in the Pursuit of "Shiny" Technologies. *Journalism Studies*, 22(14), 1987–2004.
Molyneux, L. (2015). What Journalists Retweet: Opinion, Humor, and Brand Development on Twitter. *Journalism*, 16(7), 920–935.
Molyneux, L., Holton, A., & Lewis, S. (2018). How Journalists Engage in Branding on Twitter: Individual, Organizational and Institutional Levels. *Information, Communication and Society*, 21(10), 1386–1401.
Molyneux, L., & McGregor, S. (2021). Legitimating a Platform: Evidence of Journalists' Role in Transferring Authority to Twitter. *Information, Communication & Society*. DOI: 10.1080/1369118X.2021.1874037.
Molyneux, L., & Mourão, R.R. (2019). Political Journalists' Normalization of Twitter: Interaction and new affordances. *Journalism Studies*, 20(2), 248–266.
Moore, M. (2018). *Democracy Hacked: Political Turmoil and Information Warfare in the Digital Age*. One World.
Moore, W.E. (1963). *Social Change*. Prentice-Hall, Inc.
Mounk, Y. (2018). *The People vs. Democracy: Why Our Freedom Is in Danger and How to Save It*. Harvard University Press.
Mourão, R.R. (2015). The Boys on the Timeline: Political Journalists' Use of Twitter for Building Interpretive Communities. *Journalism*, 16(8), 1107–1123.
Müller, J.W. (2017). *What Is Populism?* Penguin Books Ltd.
Murthy, D. (2013). *Twitter*. Polity Press.
Murthy, D. (2018). *Twitter* (2nd ed.). Polity Press.
Naughton, J. (2022, May 1). Elon, Twitter Is Not the Town Square – It's Just a Private Shop. The Square Belongs to Us All. *The Guardian*. https://bit.ly/3G3Rutj.
Negroponte, N. (1996). *Being Digital*. Coronet Books.
Nelson, J.L. (2021). *Imagined Audiences: How Journalists Perceive and Pursue the Public*. Oxford University Press.
Newman, N. (2021). Executive Summary and Key Findings of the 2021 Report. *Digital News Report 2021*. https://reutersinstitute.politics.ox.ac.uk/digital-news-report/2021/dnr-executive-summary.
Nielsen, R.K., & Schrøder, K.C., (2014). The Relative Importance of Social Media for Accessing, Finding, and Engaging with News. *Digital Journalism*, 2(4), 472–489.
Oschatz, C., Stier, S., & Maier, J. (2021). Twitter in the News: An Analysis of Embedded Tweets in Political News Coverage, *Digital Journalism*. DOI: 10.1080/21670811.2021.1912624.

Ottovordemgentschefelde, S. (2017). 'Organizational, Professional, Personal': An Exploratory Study of Political Journalists and Their Hybrid Brand on Twitter. *Journalism*, 18(1), 64–80.

Page, R., Barton, D., Lee, C., Wolfgang Unger, J., & Zappavigna, M. (2014). *Researching Language and Social Media: A Student Guide*. Routledge.

Papacharissi, Z. (2010). *A Private Sphere: Democracy in a Digital Age*. Polity Press.

Papacharissi, Z. (2014). *Affective Publics : Sentiment, Technology, and Politics*. Oxford University Press.

Papacharissi, Z. (2015). Towards New Journalism(s): Affective News, Hybridity, and Liminal Spaces. *Journalism Studies*, 16(1), 27–40.

Parker, G.G., van Alstyne, M.W., & Choudary, S.P. (2016). *How Networked Markets Are Transforming the Economy—and How to Make Them Work for You*. W. W. Norton & Company.

Parsons, T. (1971). *The System of Modern Societies*. Prentice-Hall.

Picard, R.G. (2014). Twilight or New Dawn of Journalism?. *Digital Journalism*, 15(5), 505–510.

Posetti, J., Aboulez, N., Bontcheva, K., Harisson, J., & Waisbord, S. (2020). *Online Violence Against Women Journalists: A Global Snapshot of Incidence and Impacts*. https://en.unesco.org/news/unescos-global-survey-online-violence-against-women-journalists.

Pukallus, S., Bradley, L., Clarke, S., & Harrison, J. (2020). From Repression to Oppression: News Journalism in Turkey 2013–2018. *Media, Culture and Society*, 42(7–8), 1443–1460.

Rashidian, N., Brown, P., & Hansen, E. (2018). Friend & Foe: The Platform Press at The Heart of Journalism. *Tow Center for Digital Journalism*. https://bit.ly/3NfE8ga.

Rashidian, N., Tsiveriotis, G., & Brown, P. (2019). Platforms and Publishers: The End of an Era. *Tow Center for Digital Journalism*. https://bit.ly/3lqrPlq.

Rauch, J. (2021). *The Constitution of Knowledge: A Defense of Truth*. Brookings Institution Press.

Revers, M. (2014). The Twitterization of News Making: Transparency and Journalistic Professionalism. *Journal of Communication*, 64, 806–826.

Revers, M. (2015). The Augmented Newsbeat: Spatial Structuring in a Twitterized News Ecosystem. *Media, Culture & Society*, 37(1), 3–18.

Robinson, J.G. (2019, June 26). The Audience in the Mind's Eye: How Journalists Imagine Their Readers. *Columbia Journalism Review*. https://www.cjr.org/tow_center_reports/how-journalists-imagine-their-readers.php.

Rogstad, I.D. (2014). Political News Journalists in Social Media. *Journalism Practice*, 8(6), 688–703.

Romanelli, El., & Tushman, M. (1994). Organizational Transformation as Punctuated Equilibrium: An Empirical Test. *The Academy of Management Journal*, 37(5), 1141–1166.

Rosen, J. (2007, June 26). The People Formerly Known as the Audience. *PressThink*. Routledge. http://archive.pressthink.org/2006/06/27/ppl_frmr.html

Roth, Y. (2022, May 19). Introducing Our Crisis Misinformation Policy. *Twitter Blog.* https://bit.ly/38belXE.
Russell, F. (2019). Twitter and News Gatekeeping. *Digital Journalism,* 7(1), 80–99.
Schudson, M., & Zelizer, B. (2017, December 15–16). Fake News in Context: In Understanding and Addressing the Disinformation Ecosystem. *Annenberg School for Communication.* https://bit.ly/3sPlqnJ.
Seymour, R. (2019). *The Twittering Machine.* The Indigo Press.
Shah, N. (2008). From Global Village to Global MarketPlace: Metaphorical Descriptions of the Global Internet. *International Journal of Media and Cultural Politics,* 4(1), 9–26.
Shapiro, I. (2014). Why Democracies Need a Functional Definition of Journalism Now More Than Ever. *Journalism Studies,* 15(5), 555–565.
Siapera, E. (2012). *Understanding New Media.* SAGE publications.
Silverstone, R. (2007). *Media and Morality: On the Rise of the Mediapolis.* Wiley.
Simon, F.M. (2019). What Determines a Journalist's Popularity on Twitter? *Journalism Studies,* 20(8), 1200–1220.
Singer, J.B. (2003). Who Are These Guys? *Journalism,* 4(2), 139–163.
Singer, J.B. (2005). The Political J-blogger: 'Normalizing' a New Media Form to Fit Old Norms and Practices. *Journalism,* 6(2), 173–198.
Smelser, N.J. (1997). *Problematics of Sociology: The Georg Simmel Lectures, 1995.* University of California Press.
Standage, T. (2013). *Writing on the Wall: Social Media - The First 2,000 Years.* Bloomsbury.
Statista (2022). https://www.statista.com/.
Stevenson, M. (2018). From Hypertext to Hype and Back Again: Exploring the Roots of Social Media in Early Web Culture. In J. Burgess, A. Marwick, & T. Poell (Eds.), *The SAGE Handbook of Social Media* (pp. 69–88). SAGE Publications.
Stone, B. (2006, August 3). *Have Your Quake and Twitter It Too.* Twitter Blog https://blog.twitter.com/en_us/a/2006/have-your-quake-and-twitter-it-too.
Stross, R. (2016, October 27). Twitter Has an Old Media Problem. Here's a Solution. *The New York Times.* https://nyti.ms/3sMujyp.
Swasy, A. (2016). *How Journalists Use Twitter: The Changing Landscape of U.S. Newsrooms.* Lexington Books.
Taleb, N.N. (2007). *The Black Swan: The Impact of the Highly Improbable.* Random House.
The New York Times (2017). *The Times Issues Social Media Guidelines for the Newsroom.* https://www.nytimes.com/2017/10/13/reader-center/social-media-guidelines.html.
Theocharis, Y., Barberá, P., Fazekas, Z., Popa, S.A., & Parnet, O. (2016). A Bad Workman Blames His Tweets: The Consequences of Citizens' Uncivil Twitter Use When Interacting with Party Candidates. *Journal of Communication,* 66, 1007–1031.
Urbinati, N. (2019). *Me the People: How Populism Transforms Democracy.* Harvard University Press.

Usher, N., Holcomb, J., & Littman, J. (2018). Twitter Makes It Worse: Political Journalists, Gendered Echo Chambers, and the Amplification of Gender Bias. *The International Journal of Press/Politics*, 23(3), 324–344.

Van der Zee, B. (2009). Twitter Triumphs. *Index on Censorship*, 38(4), 97–102.

Van Dijck, J. (2012). Tracing Twitter: The Rise of a Microblogging Platform. *International Journal of Media and Cultural Politics*, 7(3), 333–348.

Van Dijck, J. (2013). *The Culture of Connectivity*. Oxford University Press.

Van Dijck, J., Poell, T., & De Wall, M. (2018). *The Platform Society*. Oxford University Press.

Vis, F. (2013). Twitter as a Reporting Tool for Breaking News: Journalists tweeting the 2011 UK Riots. *Digital Journalism*, 1(1), 27–47.

Vollmer, H. (2013). *The Sociology of Disruption, Disaster and Social Change: Punctuated Cooperation*. Cambridge University Press.

Von Nordheim, G., Boczek, K., & Koppers, L. (2018). Sourcing the Sources: An Analysis of the Use of Twitter and Facebook as a Journalistic Source Over 10 Years in The New York Times, The Guardian, and Süddeutsche Zeitung. *Digital Journalism*, 6(7), 807–828.

Waisbord, S. (2013). *Reinventing Professionalism*. Polity Press.

Wardle, C. (2020, September 22). Understanding Information Disorder. *First Draft*. https://bit.ly/3MwDXx2.

Wardle, C., & Derakhshan, H. (2017). Information Disorder: Toward an Interdisciplinary Framework for Research and Policymaking. *Council of Europe*. https://bit.ly/3LvWdFg.

Warzel, C. (2016, August, 11). 'A Honeypot For Assholes': Inside Twitter's 10-Year Failure to Stop Harassment. *BuzzFeed News*. https://bit.ly/3G0zWOL.

Willnat L., & Weaver, D.H. (2018). Social Media and U.S. Journalists. *Digital Journalism*, 6(7), 889–909.

Wu, S., Mason, A.W., Hofman, J.M., & Watts, D.J. (2011, March 28–April 1). Who Says What to Whom on Twitter [Paper presentation]. *Proceedings of the 20th International Conference on World Wide Web*. Hyderabad, India.

Zappavigna, M. (2013). *Discourse of Twitter and Social Media: How We Use Language to Create Affiliation on the Web*. Bloomsbury Academic.

Zelizer, B. (2019). Why Journalism Is More About Than Digital Technology. *Digital Journalism*, 7(3), 343–350.

Index

Note: **Bold** page numbers refer to tables; *italic* page numbers refer to figures and page numbers followed by "n" denote endnotes.

abuse 27, 70, 73
adaption 4, 28, 32, *34*, 35, *36*, 42, 53, 57, 89, 98; *see also* short-term adaption
Alexander, J.C. 29, 31–32, 50n5
Alfaro A. 46
ambient journalism 9
ambient news environment 7–9
Amnesty International 27
Artwick, C.G. 49
audiences 20; journalist's relationship with 59–63; media 12, 37; networked 11, 23; news journalists changing nature of relationship with 59–63; news journalists proximity to 108–109

Baquet, Dean 38
Barnard, S. 18
Barnidge, M. 12, 19, 23
Barthel, M. L. 16
Barton, D. 101
Baumgartner, F.R. 4, 75, 90, 95
Baym, N. 1, 95
Bell, E. 35, 42
Boczkowski, P.J. 33–34, 39, 50n6
Bouvier, G. 27
Breton, Thierry 110n2
Broersma, M. 11, 14
Bruno, N. 12
Bruns, A. 9, 13, 48
Burgess, J. 1, 95

Canter, L. 49
Chadha, K. 18
Chadwick, A. 39
civil discourse, coarsening of 24–28
'CNN effect' 12
conventional news organisations 48
coping strategies 45–47
Cowls, J. 25, 26
Curran, J. 31
customised newspaper 9

datafication 91, 104n7
Derakhshan, H. 21
detrimental effect 27
Deuze, M. 40
Dewey, John 9
digital business card 80, 81, 107
Digital Services Act (DSA) 110n2
digital technology 31
disinformation 21, 23
disruption: as commonplace event 39–42; dimensions to 36; as displacement event 36–38; Twitter fundamentally changed news journalism 53–55
Djerf-Pierre, M. 16, 45
DSA *see* Digital Services Act (DSA)

enthusiastic activists **44**, 45
evolution 14, 32, 33, 40, 41, 75
evolutionary 3–5, 38, 30, 31, 33, 38, 40, 41, 101, 103; accounts'

122 Index

activity 89, 90; account core features **87**; adaption 35, 109; disruption 35, 109; normalisation 35, 109; punctuated equilibrium 106; timelines 75; Twitter, impact of 53–67, see also punctuated equilibrium

Facebook 1, 56–57, 63
Fink, K. 18
#FollowFriday 94, 104n8
Freedman, D. 24
free speech: absolutism 110n2; justifications 108; with regulation 109
functionalist language 43

gatewatching, two waves of 49
Gillmor (2004) 12
'global marketplace' metaphor 10–11
global village, Twitter as 10–11
Graham, T. 11, 14
Greece: news journalists, research interviews **52**, 52–53; news journalists selection 76; professional journalists from 75
greeklish 102, 104n12
Grossman, L. 6n5
Gulyas, A. 45

Harrison, J. 29
hashtags, use by journalists 91–97, *92*, *93*, *96*
Hedman, U. 16, 18, 45, 81
Hermida, A. 8, 9, 12, 22, 48
Higgins, M. 22, 26
Hodges, Dan 87
hopes 42
Horrocks, Peter 18

information disorder 21–24, 73
institution 3–5, 7, 17, 28, 29–33, 42, 43, 47, 50, 90, 105, 109
inversion process 17

Jarvis, J. 13
Java, A. 40
Johnson, K.A. 9
Johnson, M. 24
Jones, B.D. 4, 75, 90, 95

journalism: history of 32; perception as civic institution 29; technological advancement in 41
journalism crisis 12, 13, 30, 32, 33, 58, 110n2
journalistic sociality, types/forms of 10
Jukes, S. 18, 49, 97
Jungherr, A. 50n7

Kreiss, D. 29

Lasorsa, D.L. 48
Lawrence, R.G. 19
Lee, C. 101
Lee Hughes, A. 6n5
Lee, J. 15
Lewis, S.C. 27
Lieberman, M. 16, 20
long-term normalisation 31–33, *33*, 47–50
Luengo, M. 32

Madianou, M. 88
mainstream news media 25, 26
Manucci, L. 25
McGregor, S. 13, 14, 48, 49
McLuhan, M. 10
media audiences 12, 37
mediated populism 3, 7, 17, 24–28
medium-term normalisation 31–33, *33*, 47–50
Mellado, C. 46
mentions, use by journalists 91–97, *92*, *93*, *96*
meso-sociology 42
Messner, M. 18
microblogging 39–40, 51n10
Miller, D. 88
Mills, A. 6n5, 38, 51n9
Min, S.J. 18
misinformation 2, 21
Molyneux, L. 13–15, 23, 48, 49
Moore, M. 17, 24
Moore, W.E. 30, 50n1–50n4
Mourão, R.R. 23
Müller, J.W. 25
Murthy, D. 10, 40, 41, 51n10

Naughton, John 110n1, 110n2
negative feedback 90

Negroponte, N.: 'Daily Me' 9
networked audience 11, 23
networkers 45, 46
news: digitizing 33–34, *34*; gathering of 12–14
news journalism: benefits to 9, 106–107; costs to practice of 107–108; institutional framework of 42–43; institution of 3, 29–38; on intra-elite sourcing of news 49; negative effect on 74; penetration of 105; Twitter as benefiting 11–17; Twitter as distorting 17; Twitter costs and benefits to 67–74; Twitter evolution usage in 75; Twitter fundamentally changed 53–55; Twitter influence on 2
news journalism organisations 36, 38
news journalists: attitudes to Twitter 55–57; changing nature of relationship with audiences 59–63; in Chile 46; clusters of 45–46; in non-digital era 66; proximity to audience 108–109; qualitative approach, research interviews **52**, 52–53; Twitter's costs and benefits to news journalism 67–74
news journalists, Twitter account: account activity 87–91; core features of 86–87; evolutionary pattern of 88–90, *89*; formatting tweets and textual choices 97–103; of participants 76, **77–78**; participants' first Tweets (2009–2011) 76, **79–80**, 80; popularity vs. activity 88, *88*; selection of 76; tweets per journalist 88; use of hashtags 91–97, *92*, *93*, *96*; use of mentions 91–97, *92*, *93*, *96*; versions of self-presentation 80–81, **82–85**, 86
news organisations, normalisation in 47
news source, tweets as 14–15
The New York Times 38
normalisation: daily patterns of use 63–65; medium- and long-term 31–33, *33*, 47–50; reinforcement of traditional practices and networks 65–67; of Twitter 106

Obama, Barack 1, 13
official hashtags 93–94
online harassment 27
online newspapers, innovation in 33–34, *34*
opiners 45, 46
Ottovordemgentschefelde, S. 15, 80
Owen, T. 35, 42

Palen, L. 6n5
Papacharissi, Z. 37, 91
Parker, G.G. 37
Parsons, T. 30, 42, 43
personal authenticity 11
personal branding 16–17
personal touch: short-term adaption 61–63; Twitter as benefiting news journalism 15
platform press 34–35, *36*
political discourse, coarsening of 24–28
political journalism 24
populism 25; mediated 3, 7, 17, 24–28
positive feedback 90
pragmatic conformists **44**, 45
professional branding, conceptualisation of 16
professional engagement 59–61
professionalism 6n8
professional news journalism 6n8
professional pressures, Twitter effect on 17–21
promotional hashtags 94
public discourse, systematic degradation of 70
Pukallus, S. 29
punctuated equilibrium 4, 105; disruption as commonplace event 39–42; evolutionary process of 106; institution of 29–31; medium- and long-term normalisation 31–33, *33*, 47–50; online newspapers innovation 33–34, *34*; platform press 34–35, *36*; short-term adaption 31–33, *33*, 42–43, **44**, 45–47; short-term disruption 31–33, *33*, 36–38; stages of 31–38; theory of 75
punctuate equilibrium 5
punctuation disruptive events 110

qualitative analysis, on use of mentions 97, 104n10

Rashidian, N. 35
Rauch, J. 23
Rawnsley, Andrew 81
Rentoul, John 87, 101
Resnick 47
retooling 36, 50n7, 106
Revers, M. 14, 46
Rogstad, I.D. 45
Romanelli, El. 37
Rosenbaum, J. E. 27
Rosen, J. 37

sceptical shunners **44**, 45
sceptics 45–46
Schroeder, R. 25, 26
Schudson, M. 22
self-presentation, news journalists 80–81, **82–85**, 86
Seymour, R. 19, 21, 37; *The Twittering Machine* 17
short-term adaption 31–33, *33*, 42–43, **44**, 45–47; formal and informal training role in use of Twitter 57–59; journalists' attitudes to Twitter 55–57; journalist's relationship with audiences 59–63
short-term disruption 31–33, *33*, 36–38
Silverstone, R. 7
Singer, J.B. 12, 47, 48
Smelser, N.J. 29
social capital 16, 19
social change 30; argumentation about 41; complexities in 50n1; types of 50n2
social media platforms 39, 41; adaptation of 43
social media sourcing 13
social system: aspects of 50n3; complexity of 31; stability of 30; subsystem of 42
'South by Southwest' (SXSW) 1
sparks 45, 46
Sroiter, Antonis 87
Standage, T. 40
Stone, Biz 2, 8

Stross, R. 38
system 8, 31, 35, 39; awareness system 8; early warning system 2; communication systems 8, 17; media systems 9; 25; negative feedback 91; social system 30; 42

technological affordances 51n11
techno-optimism 37
textual choices, of news journalists 97–98, 101
Toffler 32, 50n5
Tow Center for Digital Journalism 34
toxicity 27, 70, 72, 73, 108
'Toxic Twitter' 27
traditional journalism 8, 25
Trump, D. 26
Tushman, M. 37
tweets, as news source 14–15
tweets, formatting of 103; commentary 99–100; commentary + link 99; headline and link 98–99; link 99; personal comments 99; personal responses 101–103; reporting 100
Twitter 1, 30, 32, 51n9; as ambient news environment 7–9; as benefiting news journalism 11–17; biography 5n1; branding self 15–17; as 'change-maker' 38; civil and political influence of 105; communicative environment 7; as distorting news journalism 17; effect on professional pressures 17–21; evaluating benefits of 67–70; evaluating costs of 70–74; evolutionary impact on news journalism 53–67; evolution usage in news journalism 75; features of 1–2; formal and informal training role in use of 57–59; as global village 10–11; idiosyncratic character 69; influence on news journalism 2; mediated populism and political and civil discourse 24–28; new audience 11–12; news gathering 12–14; news journalists attitudes to 55–57; into news organisations 43; as news source

49; as part of historical continuum 41; as part of media ecosystem 5; personal touch 15; as professional tool 55; as promotional tool 40; research on 40; safety policy 28n1; self-presentation 80–86, 103n5; techno-optimism 37; truth-seeking on 74; tweets as news source 14–15; as underpinning information disorder 21–24
Twitter agenda 18
'Twitter effect' 12–13
The Twittering Machine (Seymour) 17
Twittersphere 68
two-faced 45, 46

United Kingdom: news journalists, research interviews **52**, 52–53; news journalists selection 76; professional journalists from 75; Twittersphere 68
Urbinati, N. 25
Usher, N. 19, 24

Van der Zee, B. 6n5
Van Dijck, J. 19, 93, 104n7
'village life' metaphor 10
Vollmer, H. 31, 39
Von Nordheim, G. 24, 49
vox populi 14, 107

Wardle, C. 21
Warzel, C. 27
Waterson, Jim 87
Wells, R. 18
Williams, Evan 36

Zelizer, B. 22, 41

Taylor & Francis eBooks

www.taylorfrancis.com

A single destination for eBooks from Taylor & Francis with increased functionality and an improved user experience to meet the needs of our customers.

90,000+ eBooks of award-winning academic content in Humanities, Social Science, Science, Technology, Engineering, and Medical written by a global network of editors and authors.

TAYLOR & FRANCIS EBOOKS OFFERS:

- A streamlined experience for our library customers
- A single point of discovery for all of our eBook content
- Improved search and discovery of content at both book and chapter level

REQUEST A FREE TRIAL
support@taylorfrancis.com

For Product Safety Concerns and Information please contact our EU
representative GPSR@taylorandfrancis.com
Taylor & Francis Verlag GmbH, Kaufingerstraße 24, 80331 München, Germany

www.ingramcontent.com/pod-product-compliance
Lightning Source LLC
Chambersburg PA
CBHW051751230426
43670CB00012B/2247